Demystifying China's Stock Market

Eric Girardin • Zhenya Liu

Demystifying China's Stock Market

The Hidden Logic behind the Puzzles

Eric Girardin
Aix-Marseille University
Marseille, France

Zhenya Liu
Aix-Marseille University
Marseille, France

Renmin University of China
Beijing, China

ISBN 978-3-030-17122-3   ISBN 978-3-030-17123-0   (eBook)
https://doi.org/10.1007/978-3-030-17123-0

This Palgrave Pivot imprint is published by the registered company Springer Nature Switzerland AG.
The registered company address is: Gewerbestrasse 11, 6330 Cham, Switzerland

PREFACE

The world fund management industry is eyeing the opening of China's stock market as its new frontier. China's fund management industry is about to become the second largest in the world, while its current products are heavily tilted towards low-margin money market funds. China's rising middle class has to save a lot to protect itself against its own risk of unemployment, as well as for retirement, healthcare, and the education of its children. The overall value of bank deposits plus investments and insurance products had reached $19 trillion in late 2017 and should rise by one fourth by the end of 2019. The authorities in China have been gradually relaxing the constraints on domestic stock market investment faced by financial institutions, including asset management by large banks' subsidiaries and insurance companies. They aim at increasing the participation of professional 'long-term' investors to dampen market volatility generated by retail trades. In particular, foreign fund management groups can help reinforce China's institutional asset management industry to further moderate the influence of sentiment-driven individual stock market investors.

Questions abound with respect to the incentives faced by investors who consider investing in China's stock market. What is the optimal detention period for stock? Is it advisable to trade very frequently or rather to buy-and-hold over decades as recommended by Siegel (2014) for a large number of markets? Should investors rather stick to short- or medium-run horizons? These are questions which matter both for domestic investors, who represent the bulk of stock trading in China, and for foreign investors for whom the Chinese stock market often operates like a magnet.

In 2020, China's stock markets are going to celebrate their 30th anniversary. Within such a short lifetime, the transformations have been stunning, from a minnow with only 8 listed companies to the second largest capitalization at the global scale, with close to 3500 listed firms. From less than 4% of Gross Domestic Product (GDP) in 1992, the stock market capitalization equalled the value of annual GDP precisely 15 years later, in Summer 2007, even if it was scaled down to 66% in 2017. China's stock market index has just been included in the MSCI Emerging Market Index. The process of development from small and regional stock markets into a national unified stock market thus took only a few decades in China, while it had taken one or two hundred years in many developed countries.

The spectacular expansion in stock market size and scope has been driven both by the supply and demand sides. The former has included the acceleration in the pace of corporate restructuring, the privatization of state-owned enterprises, and the listing of new ventures. The latter has stemmed from an increased participation of financial institutions and a gradual seasoning of individual investors. China's stock markets have developed into a marketplace whose legal system, trading rules, and regulatory frameworks seem aligned with international standards and principles; such features are crucial for attracting foreign portfolio investment.

The major difficulty met by any attempt to understand the Chinese stock market is due to the enormous distance between such appearances and reality. This shows in two ways. First, the progress made in the legal framework may not have made much difference since enforcement has not substantially improved. Second, standard tools for the assessment of either valuation or performance are of little use when the earnings, the book value of assets, and the market price of firms are manipulated by different sets of multiple principals interacting at both central and deconcentrated levels of government. Foreign observers attempting to rationalize observed movements in China's stock market, and foreign investors keen to invest in that market, should attempt to see through appearances and disentangle such a complex web of interactions.

Most existing books in English on China's stock markets have been exclusively written with a single perspective, that of practitioners (Green 2003; Walter and Howie 2001, 2006), of regulators (Neftçi et al. 2007; Cheng et al. 2015), or of quantitative analysts (Groenewold et al. 2004), and most of the time have only dealt with the initial decade of the market. Chinese-language literature is generally rather descriptive and mainly geared towards the regulator's point of view or that of the general public.

It is necessary not only to combine the different approaches, using both empirical and theoretical tools, but also to take into account the decisive progress made in the research field in the last decade. Western accounting and finance research, which initially gauged the Chinese stock market against global standards, with tools developed for OECD markets, and thus uncovered numerous puzzles (Carpenter and Whitelaw 2015; Allen et al. 2014), belatedly acknowledges the necessity to change perspective. This points to going beyond a benchmarking of China's market against an often inadequate template (Carpenter and Whitelaw 2017; Wong 2016), focusing on what this market lacks, and searching instead for its internal specific logic, concerned with finding what this market is.

Though it would thus be tempting to leave aside the template offered by the universal economic and financial principles and focus simply on the Chinese characteristics, it seems more fruitful to adopt a more pragmatic approach, focusing on how reform worked rather than on why it worked, as advised by Qian (2017). Such an approach should pay a lot of attention to initial historical conditions and experience, as well as to contemporary constraints.

To that effect one needs in particular to examine the historical experience of the early organization of companies, as well as of interpersonal relations, in imperial China (Faure 2006) and the first experience of China with a stock market from the late Qing empire to the eve of the PRC (Thomas 2001). Using the lessons of agency theory, one also needs to go behind the apparent convergence of China's laws and regulations to global standards and understand the actual specific enforcement mechanisms (Chen 2013), as well as account for the multitask character of state-owned firms (Bai et al. 2000), and the political economy of the complex interplay of multiple principals at many geographical levels of government at work in the functioning of China's stock market.

For the stock market, as in many other aspects of modern China, the experience gathered during the late Qing imperial regime has left deep traces. This is particularly the case for China's ever-reappearing Phoenix-like stock market, which, in recurrent ways, arose and was closed and reopened in a different guise. Indeed, as we show in Chap. 2, many lessons from China's first stock market have been mirrored, sometimes in a polar way, in the design of China's modern stock market. The imbalance between the domestic and international segments of the market, and its speculative character, are such enduring features. It is noteworthy that on the eve of the Second World War, Shanghai's stock market was one of the leading stock exchanges in Asia. After a lasting hibernation period, and in the wake of the deep reforms of the late 1970s and early 1980s, the re-emergence of share issuance and trading was active, rather spontaneous, and somewhat hectic. It initially corresponded with the decentralized nature of industrial expansion during that period, but soon left room to the local-governments-initiated restructuring of some enterprises into shareholding companies. In the absence of any organized stock exchange, over-the-counter transactions resulted in a highly speculative and decentralized market.

It is tempting to view the design of China's modern stock market from the perspective of the financial development paradigm, which recommends emerging economies to insert such a market design within the agenda of domestic and external financial liberalization, with a neat sequencing where markets are deemed to play an increasingly dominant role. We will see in Chap. 3 that this perspective, while undoubtedly useful, must be tempered by two other major frameworks. The first one is the latecomer's perspective, which acknowledges that, in economies engaged in catching up, state intervention may have to play a decisive role in the framing of the financial system. The second one is the transition character of China's economy, the conduct of which has been set within a 'socialist market economy'. In the absence of any template, either from theory or from historical experience, for inserting a stock market within such a socialist market economy, China has gradually shaped its own model, where it is not surprising to find that the stock market is dominated by the government. To some extent the privatization process went some way towards damping such domination, even though it may have remained in place in a different guise.

China's stock market is characterized by major anomalies, often called puzzles, implying large departures from an informationally-efficient market, which we will examine in Chap. 4. First, the specific characteristics of China's stock market (at least initially and still to a large extent) fit(ted) the combination of ingredients which, theory tells us, lead to a speculative market with recurrent bubbles: short-sale constraints, the domination of individual investors, a reduced float, and often costly (or impossible) arbitrage. Idiosyncratic seasonalities represent the second recurrent anomaly. A Red-May effect, with the highest returns around that month every year, stands in sharp contrast to the January effect which rules in most major stock markets, and may be linked in China to the seasonal behaviour of credit awarded by banks. Third, the segmentation across markets involves a higher price of the domestic-listed versus the foreign-listed shares of Chinese mainland companies, an opposite premium to that characterizing multiple listings of other countries' companies. It is a puzzle which repeated timid attempts by China's authorities at moving away from a rigid currency peg or at the gradual lifting of capital controls have not been able to suppress.

The full implications of the government domination of China's stock market can only be understood within a modern political economy perspective. We will highlight in Chap. 5 how the dynamics of China's stock market is fundamentally driven by core characteristics of the organization of the state-owned enterprise sector and the complex institutional apparatus. The divide between appearances and reality will be sharply illustrated, in an analysis of corporate governance, with the gap between a modernized legal framework and serious limits to its enforcement. The major political economy feature of the Chinese stock market is the multiplicity of principals in the agency process, at the central like at three distinct local levels. This process initially took place in the listing of companies, that is, the primary market, and subsequently moved to the secondary market. In sum, the government did not intend to build a complete stock market but was keen to use this market as a politico-economic instrument and keep everything under control. Incompleteness of the stock market is the natural product of government dominance.

The new argument developed in this book will not be based on original research but both on existing research reported in published literature with academic references, and on new descriptive empirical evidence. We will use publicly available data on China's stock market and economy, mentioning the sources. This work is the product of our individual and joint research on China's stock market over recent decades, as well as of first-hand experience of this market both as a practitioner and as a regulator for one of us.

We benefited a lot from discussions and interactions with many scholars and market participants. Recurring visits to many institutions helped us deepen our understanding of the complexity of the market. We would like to thank especially for their hospitality the Asian Development Bank Institute, the Bank for International Settlements (Asia-Pacific office), the Chinese Academy of Social Sciences (Beijing), the Institute of Transition of the Bank of Finland, the Graduate School of the People's Bank of China, the Hong Kong Institute of Monetary Research, and Fudan and Renmin Universities.

We would like to thank our colleagues and friends, such as Joe Fung, Christian Henriot, William Marois, Jacques Melitz, Georges Prat, Eli Remolona, Xiaoqiu Wu, and Yanrui Wu, who were kind enough to spare some time to read an early draft of this book, and we hope that the final version will be closer to their wishes. The suggestions provided by two anonymous reviewers have been very constructive and especially helpful. Palgrave's staff has been of continuous support during the whole process of the writing of this book, and we are especially grateful to Laura Pacey and Clara Heathcock for their gentle pressure and their efficiency. Finally, it is only thanks to the patience and understanding of our families that we were able to spend time at, and away from, home to carry out this work.

Marseille, France   Eric Girardin
Beijing, China   Zhenya Liu

REFERENCES

Allen, F. J. Qian, S.C. Shan, and J.L. Zhu. 2014. The Best Performing Economy with the Worst Performing Stock Market: Explaining the Poor Performance of the Chinese Stock Market. Manuscript, Imperial College, University of London.

Bai, C.-E., D. Li, Z. Tao, and Y. Wang. 2000. A Multitask Theory of State Enterprise Reform. *Journal of Comparative Economics* 28: 716–738.

Carpenter, J.N., F. Lu, and R.F. Whitelaw. 2015. The Real Value of China's Stock Market. NBER Working Paper, 20957.

Carpenter, J.N., and R.F. Whitelaw. 2017. The Development of China's Stock Market and Stakes for the Global Economy. *Annual Review of Financial Economics* 9: 233–257.

Chen, D. 2013. *Corporate Governance Enforcement and Financial Development: The Chinese Experience*. Cheltenham: Edward Elgar.

Cheng, S., and Z. Li. 2015. *The Chinese Stock Market*. Vol. 2. Basingstoke: Palgrave Macmillan.

Faure, D. 2006. *China and Capitalism: A History of Business Enterprise in Modern China*. Hong Kong: Hong Kong University Press.

Green, S. 2003. *China's Stock Market: A Guide to its Progress, Players and Prospects*. London: Profile Books.

Groenewold, N.S., Y. Wu, H.K. Tanang, and X.M. Fan. 2004. *The Chinese Stock Market: Efficiency, Predictability and Profitability*. Cheltenham: Edward Elgar.

Neftçi, S.N. and M. Y. Menager-Xu. eds. 2007. *China's Financial Markets: An Insider's Guide to How the Markets Work*. Burlington: Elsevier.

Qian, Y. 2017. *How Reform Worked in China: The Transition from Plan to Market.* Cambridge, MA: MIT Press.

Siegel, J. 2014. *Stocks for the Long Run: The Definitive Guide to Financial Market Returns and Long-Term Investment Strategy.* New York: McGraw-Hill.

Thomas, A.W. 2001. *Western Capitalism in China: A History of the Shanghai Stock Exchange.* Aldershot: Ashgate.

Walter, C.E., and F.J.T. Howie. 2001. *'To Get Rich is Glorious': China's Stock Markets in the '80s and '90s.* Basingstoke: Palgrave.

Walter, C.E., and F.J.T. Howie. 2006. *Privatizing China: Inside China's Stock Markets.* Singapore: Wiley.

Wong, T.J. 2016. Corporate Governance Research on Listed Firms in China. *Foundations and Trends in Accounting* 9 (4): 259–326.

CONTENTS

About the Authors

Eric Girardin studied at Paris-Sorbonne and Cambridge Universities, is affiliated with the School of Economics at Aix-Marseille University, and is visiting professor at Beijing-University-H.S.B.C. Business School (UK). He has supervised a dozen PhD students on China's economy and financial system. He has conducted research on China for the Asian Development Bank, the Asian Development Bank Institute, the Bank for International Settlements, the European Commission, and the OECD Development Centre. He has held frequent visiting positions with the Bank of Finland Institute on Transition, the Chinese Academy of Social Sciences, Fudan University, the Hong Kong Institute for Monetary Research, and the Graduate School of the People's Bank of China. He was a member of the Advisory Council of the Asian Development Bank Institute and sits on the board of the China Economic Association (EU). He coordinated an EU-Marie Curie research contract on China's Electricity Industry. His 75 publications include 20 journal articles on China's stock, real estate, and foreign exchange markets. He wrote a monograph on *Banking Sector Reform and Credit Control in China*, OECD, in 1997, showing early on the dangers of an uncontrolled development of non-bank financial institutions.

Zhenya Liu accumulated experience as an academic at the School of Finance, Renmin University of China and University of Birmingham. He is a regulator and a financial market practitioner, director of the board of JP Morgan Futures (China), and Chairman of Hedge Funds in Beijing and Hong Kong. He has supervised more than 20 PhD theses on China's financial system, with graduates employed with the Ministry of Finance, People's Bank of China, CBRC, and within China's finance industry, as well as UK universities. He has written more than 20 books in Chinese and 50 publications both in Chinese and English on the Chinese economic and financial system, especially the stock market, including *Shareholding System and Limited Company* (1992) and *Securities Investment and Investment Techniques* (1993).

The two authors have been engaged in joint work on China's stock market since 2000, as testified by published articles in the leading journals in the field, *China Economic Review*, the US Chinese Economists' Society's journal; the *Journal of Chinese Economic and Business Studies*, the UK/EU China Economic Association's journal.

LIST OF FIGURES

LIST OF TABLES

CHAPTER 1

Demystifying China's Stock Market: The Hidden Logic Behind the Puzzles

Abstract Mainstream research has rationalized China's stock market on the basis of paradigms such as the institutional approach, the efficient market hypothesis, and corporate valuation principles. The deviations from such paradigms have been analysed as puzzles of China's stock market. However, "research on China's financial system should avoid over-applying research paradigms developed for the US setting" (Carpenter and Whitelaw, The Development of China's Stock Market and Stakes for the Global Economy. Manuscript, New York Stern School of Business, June 2017). We will explore to what extent, far from being puzzles, these 'deviations' are rather the symptoms of a consistent strategy for the design, development, and regulation of a government-dominated financial system with Chinese characteristics.

The main characteristics of the Chinese stock market stem from its historical origins, development process and internal logic. The earliest Shanghai stock market appeared around 1865. It was foreign dominated both for issuers and investors, who were mostly individuals. China's modern stock market largely inherited the speculative character of the early stock market.

The most striking feature of the modern market is government domination. The government aims at using the stock market to solve the long-term financing problem of state-owned enterprises. Therefore, this stock market is very different from the stock market of developed countries, generating the so-called "puzzles" in Westerners' views. The dominance

© The Author(s) 2019   1
E. Girardin, Z. Liu, *Demystifying China's Stock Market*,
https://doi.org/10.1007/978-3-030-17123-0_1

of political economy features, involving multiple principals, and the large gap between advanced regulations and poor enforcement, are the major sources of incompleteness of the Chinese stock market.

Keywords Chinese stock market • Internal logic • Puzzles • History • Government-domination

1.1   THE PUZZLES

This chapter provides the motivations and objectives of the book. It identifies three core characteristics, corresponding to as many chapters, and presents the rationale behind their interconnections. The three core characteristics are: the domination of the market by China's government and administrative apparatus; the inherent speculative character of the market; and the wide departure from the standard template of stock-market organization and functioning.

The main message here is that government involvement is key to an understanding of the, often surprising, characteristics of the market. We will argue that the strategy used by the government to build the stock market has been based on the need to gradually set up the increasingly complex financing channels of a growing emerging economy; an economy initially dominated by state-owned enterprises (SOEs), which was subsequently marketized and liberalized. Such a strategy was constrained by the persistent willingness to keep these processes under tight control.

As a by-product of its design this market is inherently speculative in character. This is reflected in recurrent bubbles, mostly separated by bearish episodes. A similar degree of government involvement is apparent in its stop-and-go policies which aim both at using the market and trying to tame it.

The departures from the features of a 'complete' market are so numerous that it is doubtful that the latter has been used as a template by the Chinese authorities. Investors have no true ownership of the companies they hold shares in. As a result, they are not involved, let alone interested, in governance. Moreover, since for many years the distribution of dividends was at best erratic and at worst nonexistent, the holding of shares by many (especially retail) investors has had by nature a speculative character, relying almost exclusively on expected capital gains. The published earnings have no clear relationship with stock prices since they do not reflect the profitability of firms.

Western scholars often benchmark the features of China's stock market against global standards. The researcher's attention thus always tends to focus on what the Chinese market lacks, rather than on how it is designed and actually functions. A full understanding of the Chinese stock market requires an analysis of the market on its own terms rather than by reference to a misleading benchmark (Li and Milhaupt 2013).

1.2   THE PHOENIX MARKET

We will look at the historical experience of China with stock markets over the last century and a half in Chap. 2. In a Phoenix-like fashion the stock market in Shanghai disappeared and reappeared several times. It is essential to look back to the immediate and remote ancestors of the modern Chinese stock market to grasp its specific features.

To understand the origins of the organization of companies in China, it is necessary to go back even further in time and review the forms of companies that emerged in imperial China in the late Ming dynasty, which ruled until 1644. Unlike Western companies, early Chinese business organizations were based on lineages and rules. Such lineage relationships lasted much longer than any form of business partnership and reflected collective ownership at multiple levels. This arrangement played a big role in the creation of some early forms of Chinese joint stock companies.

Although the central government of imperial China centralized power, the use of the market to provide financing for industrial/commercial enterprises was not its concern. However, Chinese entrepreneurs could still use an organizational structure similar to that of western companies and securities transactions to finance enterprises. The salt field in Zigong, in Sichuan province (Zelin 2005) and the Shandong Agricultural Company (Pomeranz 1997) were good examples of such a use.

The first Chinese stock market, in the late nineteenth century, was segmented between domestic and foreign participants, both for firms in the listing process and for investors. Listing was Treaty-port driven, which means heavily dominated by foreign firms, and investors were mainly China-based foreign residents.

The incompleteness of the market as well as its speculative nature, core features of the modern market, were already inherent characteristics of the

Shanghai stock market during the 1865 to 1911 period. Government involvement was not a major feature initially under the late Qing dynasty but certainly played an increasing role, especially in the subsequent republican period.

A striking feature of the Shanghai stock market is its resilience, that is, its ability to often disappear and reappear, in a different shape, some time later. The longest period of extinction was experienced in the first four decades of the PRC, but this had been preceded by shorter interruptions in the first half of the twentieth century. In 1914 the new Republic of China issued the Security Exchange Law. In 1916 in Shanghai, Sun Yat-sen set up the Shanghai Stocks and Commodities Exchange and tried to fund the government by issuing bonds. The government of Yuan Shikai, in North China, set up its own Beijing Stock Exchange. In 1920 only Shanghai's stock market remained in operation. Later on, Chiang Kai-chek closed the exchange which the Japanese had created in the early 1940s and, in September 1946, his government set up a new Shanghai Stock Exchange, which would be closed by the PRC.

Recurring speculative episodes were followed by equally large crashes, which dampened investors' appetite for shares for decades, and this in turn was followed by a persistently depressed market. Dividend distribution was rather strange: it had no direct relationship with earnings but was regular and based on some magic fixed numbers. Accordingly, shares were often akin to bonds.

Government intervention took different forms during the period of the late Qing dynasty on the one hand and in the Republican period on the other. In the former period, companies were initially founded through the 'government-controlled and merchant-managed' scheme, though private ones appeared in the late 1890s; post-1911 government intervention was at times heavy.

In the PRC, as a by-product of the economic reforms of the late 1970s and early 1980s, there was a spontaneous re-emergence of share issuance and trading. The decentralized nature of industrial expansion during that period, in the form of a shareholding cooperative system for collective and small state-owned enterprises, was based on unregulated private placements, with no formal exchange. The landmark industrial reforms of the mid 1980s gave a decisive impetus to the restructuring of some enterprises into shareholding companies. The stock market during that time suffered from the lack of any unified national regulation and supervision. Accordingly the multiple informal exchanges remained very hectic, very speculative, as they even involved investors in lottery-type primary markets.

1.3   A FINANCIAL SYSTEM DOMINATED BY THE GOVERNMENT

The dominance of the government has been the driving force of the design and development of a financial system with Chinese characteristics, and the creation of the stock market can only be understood as one of the stages of the creation/development of that financial system.

The motivations behind the transformation in the channels of financing of the economy, after the reform initiated late 1978, help understand the logic behind the design of the financial system. Initially the financing of SOEs relied exclusively on subsidies. The 1984 reform involved a shift to loan financing by the newly-created four state owned banks. Household savings deposited with banks became the privileged source of firms' (indirect) external finance. In a similar way as the subsidies received by state-sector firms were previously not expected to be repaid, it is not obvious that SOEs should have been expected to repay the bank loans they received.

In the 1980s, SOE managers had little ex post autonomy because the enterprise committee was ultimately responsible for management decisions (Naughton 1996). There was an attempt in the late 1980s to let SOEs sort their own problems by themselves, which was associated with the slogan "self-management and self-responsibility". State-ownership remained, but managers and employees would share in the good or bad performance. With the 1988 Enterprise Law, the SOE manager signed a contract with the relevant state entity, thus giving him or her some rights on profits and losses. Ideally the manager would then be motivated to reward workers with incentive-based payments (Cauley and Sandler 1992, 2001). However, such reforms failed to change the behaviour of firms, and proper payments as reward for performance were never provided to workers by managers. In this perspective, it may not be surprising that the low-efficiency SOEs very soon created huge non-performing loans (NPLs), burdening the state-owned banking sector.

After deep thinking about the possible ways forward, a new quick fix was soon discovered. The government then believed that the creation of the stock market would improve both the corporate finance of SOEs and their efficiency. The creation of the share market in the early 1990s partly shifted firms' financing from an intermediated to a direct form, again relying (now directly) on household savings. At the same time the listing of banks enabled them to shift part of the burden of NPLs to a new source of financing.

In Chap. 3 we will also discuss the stages of development of the market from 1990 onwards, with the privatization of small- and medium-sized SOEs (while keeping large ones under state ownership), the split-share reform which brought the float closer to capitalization, and the opening and deepening of the market. The gradual character of market design will also be illustrated by the study of the recent stages of reforms.

The heavy involvement of the government has been strongly felt in the design and enforcement of regulation, as well as in the supervision of the market. New market creation was dominated by the regulator, the China Securities and Regulatory Commission (CSRC), which is part of the government administrative structure. The regulator played a major role in the creation, in the late 2000s-early 2010s, of the Small and Medium Enterprises board, the Second Board for high-tech companies (ChiNext), and the Stock Index Futures. In addition, the CSRC directly intervened in the creation, control, or restructuring, of large institutional investors, such as hedge funds or mutual funds and intermediaries, such as security companies.

1.4   A SPECULATIVE MARKET

In Chap. 4 we will assess the factors attracting Chinese investors to the stock market as well as the optimal detention period for stocks. Individual investors lack alternative investment opportunities. Household holding of domestic government bonds became unpopular due to forced holding and the upheavals in the bond market in the first half of the 1990s. Moreover, for long, the capital market was all but closed. Given the general lack of financial expertise of such individual investors, it is no surprise that their decisions would be driven by sentiment, leading to waves of extreme upward and downward movements. The volatility of sentiment has been enhanced by the indirect intervention of the government apparatus in the market through the media, as well as through rule issuance or cancelation.

The theoretical framework provided by Scheinkman and Xiong (2003) and Hong et al. (2006) shows that, in the presence of both heterogeneous beliefs and short-sale constraints, investors may be induced to overpay for an asset if they expect to sell it to another investor who will be willing to pay even more in the future. The dominance of unsophisticated investors, binding short-sale constraints, and, often costly, arbitrage characterized the stock market in mainland China, at least in the 1990s. Accordingly, it is not surprising that such a market would be speculative.

Direct government regulation, particularly through stop-and-go IPO (initial public offering) policies is yet another factor producing a very volatile market. Indeed, the CSRC alternatively decides the timing, magnitude and nature of IPOs, or their lengthy discontinuation, often generating discrete jumps in prices (Allen et al. 2014). The stock market waves are themselves fuelled or interrupted by the frequent alternations of loose and restrictive monetary policy, often motivated by the attempt to repeatedly stimulate or cool down the stock market.

Anomalies are associated with a rather specific sequence of stock market phases: short bull episodes, long bear markets (persisting up to 5 or 6 years), with recurrent bubbles in between. We will argue, for example, that the 2014–2015 bubble and crash, far from showing that the stock market got out of control, rather illustrate the dangers of a too hands-on approach. The government talked up and fuelled the up-side and subsequently stopped the play itself. Margin trading and high leverage amplified the bubble, but in no way initiated it. A coordinated strategy by the different authorities would have been able to prevent, or at least sharply moderate, the upheavals.

The analysis of the operation of China's stock market usually emphasizes that three main anomalies are related to deviations from the EMH. First, the bubbles that often occur in the market are the most important anomaly. This anomaly is related to major features of the market, such as government stop-and-go policies, a large proportion of initially immature individual investors, no (or limited) short-selling mechanisms, and high arbitrage costs. The distinctive seasonality is the second recurrent anomaly. The highest returns in the year occur in the spring in China, the so-called Red-May effect, in stark contrast to the January effect of stock markets in most developed countries. The Red-May effect seems to be related to the seasonal pattern of bank credit and industrial production. Third, due to China's almost closed capital account, the share price of domestic listed companies is usually much above their overseas listed stock prices. Such a premium is the so-called 'puzzle' of the Chinese stock market, with a positive premium opposite to the negative one which characterizes the share price of multiple-listed firms of other countries. We will argue that such anomalies, which can look like puzzles of the Chinese stock market, may rather be the natural products of major characteristics of that market.

1.5   THE POLITICAL ECONOMY OF AN INCOMPLETE MARKET

There is sharp disagreement between on the one hand the accounting view, based on corporate valuation analysis, which considers that valuation in China's stock market has reached standards similar to that of the US stock market (Carpenter et al. 2015), and on the other hand financial system scholars who find a sharp disconnect between the stock market and the economy, noting that China has "the best performing economy with the worst performing stock market" (Allen et al. 2014). In Chap. 5 we will show that the Chinese stock market departs in four major ways from the typical template of advanced countries' markets (as acknowledged partly in the survey by Carpenter and Whitelaw 2017), yielding a 'Chinese-style' corporate governance system. First, even if many regulations have been brought into line with global standards, their enforcement still features a large number of idiosyncratic characteristics. Second, concentration of ownership has plagued both state- and privately-owned firms. Third, actual earnings have been distorted by the high interest rates charged by state-owned banks for loans, and reported earnings have been massaged by firms prior to (and after) listing, generating a loose relationship between current stock prices and future earnings. Fourth, different sets of multiple principals interact at both central and deconcentrated[1] levels of government to independently manipulate not only earnings but also the book value of assets and the stock market prices. We will argue that the characteristics of a governance system in China, which differs strongly from western standards, are not mechanically associated with an opportunistic

---

[1] Deconcentration, which refers to the dispersion of control within one single organization, is more adapted to the Chinese setting than the, often used, concept of decentralization, which rather refers to the transfer of control from one organization to another (Lemieux 2008; Aritonang 2016). This can be linked to the distinction made by Gu Yanwu in his 1660 essay on the "Prefectural System" (see Kuhn 1975), between *Junxian*, referring to the division of the Chinese empire among administrative jurisdictions (prefectures, counties) governed by centrally appointed and rotated officials, and *Fengjian*, in which local elites govern localities.

behaviour by the managers of firms but can be rationalized as optimal responses to the very specific institutional context in which firms operate.

Contrary to a dominant view, the liberalization or opening of the Chinese financial system is not aimed at endangering the dominance of the stock market by the government. They represent the only means by which extra sources of finance are provided to firms, but always at the margin. Investors use the stock market to get speculative returns, so they have little wish, or incentive, to exercise governance or to insist on more information disclosure. Firms use the stock market to get extra finance and are not interested in benefiting from a complete market fulfilling its usual functions.

Overall the government did not intend to build a complete stock market. For a complete market to arise, individuals would need to become true investors. Listed SOEs would need to become genuine firms answering directly to all shareholders and to completely stop fulfilling their social functions. The government does not want the market to provide market signals because the authorities believe, rightly or wrongly, that they are able to provide better signals, avoiding market chaos. The market is a politico-economic instrument, not a standard market.

The book will have shown that the stock market in China fits within a financial system which has been gradually (and sometimes discontinuously) designed in a way (at least ex post) consistent with the agenda of the authorities. It does fulfil some functions, such as compelling SOEs to become more transparent, competitive and externally monitored.

In the light of our argument it is unlikely that the Chinese government would allow, in the near future, full ownership by private investors, full disclosure, full liberalization and full external opening. Incompleteness is going to stay for a substantial time. This yields an original and unique mix of market and state-directed financial system, where the former is apparently playing an increasing role, subject to the preferences and agenda of the government.

REFERENCES

Allen, F., J. Qian, S.C. Shan, and J.L. Zhu. 2014. The Best Performing Economy with the Worst Performing Stock Market: Explaining the Poor Performance of the Chinese Stock Market. Manuscript, Imperial College, University of London.

Aritonang, D.M. 2016. Politics of Deconcentration for Local Government: The Case of Indonesia. *Journal of Law, Policy and Globalization* 55: 79–86.

Carpenter, J.N., F. Lu, and R.F. Whitelaw. 2015. The Real Value of China's Stock Market. NBER Working Paper, 20957.

Carpenter, J.N., and R.F. Whitelaw. 2017. The Development of China's Stock Market and Stakes for the Global Economy. Manuscript, New York Stern School of Business, June.

Cauley, J., and T. Sandler. 1992. Agency Theory and the Chinese Enterprise Reform. *China Economic Review* 3: 39–56.

———. 2001. Agency Costs and the Crisis of China's SOEs. *China Economic Review* 12: 293–297.

Hong, H., J. Scheinkman, and W. Xiong. 2006. Asset Float and Speculative Bubbles. *Journal of Finance* 61: 1073–1117.

Kuhn, P.A. 1975. Local Self-government Under the Republic: Problems of Controls, Autonomy and Mobilization. In *Conflict and Control in Late Imperial China*, ed. F. Wakeman Jr. and C. Grant, 257–298. Berkeley: University of California Press.

Lemieux, V. 2008. Deconcentration and Decentralization: A Question of Terminology. *Canadian Public Administration* 29 (2): 318–323.

Li, L.W., and C.J. Milhaupt. 2013. We are the (National) Champions: Understanding the Mechanisms of State Capitalism in China. *Stanford Law Review* 65 (4): 697–760.

Naughton, B. 1996. *Growing Out of the Plan: Chinese Economic Reform, 1978–1993*. Cambridge: Cambridge University Press.

Pomeranz, K. 1997. Traditional Chinese Business Forms Revisited: Family, Firm, and Financing in the History of the Yutang Company of Jining, 1779–1956. *Late Imperial China* 18: 1–38.

Scheinkman, J., and W. Xiong. 2003. Overconfidence and Speculative Bubbles. *Journal of Political Economy* 111: 1183–1219.

Zelin, M. 2005. *The Merchants of Zigong: Industrial Entrepreneurship in Early Modern China*. New York: Columbia University Press.

CHAPTER 2

What Does History Tell Us? The Roots of China's Modern Stock Market

Abstract An understanding of many, somewhat surprising, features of China's modern stock market and company organization requires a deep historical perspective on traditions dating back to imperial China. We will look at the form in which the corporation arose early on in imperial China in order to identify examples of well-functioning shareholding enterprises, understand the specific nature of contracting relationships, and explore the antecedents of sophisticated financial markets.

After its emergence in the late 1860s, China's first stock market developed its own specific features which are still relevant, sometimes in a mirrored way, for China's modern stock market. Domestic issuers and investors were not treated on equal terms with foreign ones. The market was characterized by durable speculative or bearish episodes badly damaging the trust of investors. During the post-1911 period, bearish phases were frequent and the government was quite often involved, in particular, to set up or discontinue exchanges.

In the wake of the deep reforms of the late 1970s and early 1980s, the re-emergence of share issuance and trading was active, rather spontaneous and somewhat hectic. It initially corresponded with the decentralized nature of industrial expansion during that period which took the form of a shareholding cooperative system for collective and small state-owned enterprises. There was no formal exchange but unregulated private placements. The landmark industrial reforms of the mid 1980s gave a decisive impetus to the restructuring of some enterprises into shareholding

© The Author(s) 2019

E. Girardin, Z. Liu, *Demystifying China's Stock Market*,

https://doi.org/10.1007/978-3-030-17123-0_2

companies. There were some unregulated exchanges in large cities but transactions were mainly over-the-counter in a myriad of localities, leading to a highly speculative market.

The design of China's modern stock market deliberately or unconsciously built on lessons drawn from the first Chinese stock market in three dimensions. First, the speculative character is a common feature, with the domination of individual investors for whom fundamentals do not play a major role. Second, the use of capital markets to provide financing to the government and state-controlled firms is shared between the old and the new markets. Third, incompleteness of the market is still present but for opposite reasons; it is a market dominated by domestic issuers and investors as opposed to earlier foreign dominance.

Keywords History • Government intervention • Chinese culture • Phoenix market • Stock market's origins

2.1   INTRODUCTION

To understand the historical environment of modern China's stock market, it is important to look back at the form in which the corporation arose early on in imperial China, to identify early examples of well-functioning shareholding enterprises, and to explore the antecedents of sophisticated financial markets. During this presentation we will need to emphasize the specific nature of contracting relationships in imperial China, which took a very different form to what is familiar in Continental European and Anglo-Saxon countries. The tension between the Chinese tradition of relationship-based or personal rules of business transactions and formal structures of governance and contracting will resurface repeatedly in the history of China's stock markets (Chen 2006).

In this chapter, we will also look at the historical experience of China with stock markets over the last century and a half. In a Phoenix-like fashion, the stock market in Shanghai has been disappearing and reappearing several times. It is essential to examine the immediate and remote ancestors of the modern Chinese stock market to understand its specific features. The modern market borrowed from the first market, initiated in the 1860s, either replicating some of its characteristics, like a highly speculative nature, or taking the polar opposite to some other features, like the dominance of domestic issuers and investors as opposed to the dominance of foreign ones in the old market. The modern market also shares with the Shanghai market during part of the post-1911 period, a heavy government involvement, while the hands-off approach which characterized the late Qing government's behaviour towards the market was echoed in the 1980s.

The multiple major changes which make the PRC apparently very different both from the late Qing and the republican periods, would lead observers to expect that the modern stock market would share very few features with its ancestors. However, the designers of China's modern securities market deliberately or unconsciously absorbed some of the experience of the first Chinese stock markets and formed a market with two characteristics: speculation, and at times heavy government-involvement. Due to the many collapses in the history of China's securities market, investors initially believed, in the 1990s, that the modern securities market may not last for a very long time, leading to short-termism. Later on, the lack of dividend distribution and the sharp market reversals reinforced such short-termism.

The economic reforms of the late 1970s and early 1980s very soon made it urgent to extend the reforms to the financial system in order to provide sufficient financing to the newly-created collective enterprises or the reformed small state-owned enterprises (SOEs). Such financial reform led to a quite inventive combination of bank loans, bond and share issuance, in which financial products were often hybrids of those three assets. The training period of the 1980s is also instructive, in as much as the informal nature of the competing multiple markets quickly led the authorities to realize the necessity both of unifying regulation and supervision, and of setting up formal exchanges.

2.2 Corporations, Shareholding, and Early Financial Markets in Imperial China

2.2.1 First Corporations and Shareholding Enterprises

At about the same time as Europe, China went through a commercial revolution in the sixteenth century, but unlike the former, did not develop an ideology based on individualism which would make its way into business (Faure 2006). In a very different way, China was characterized by the discovery of the power of ritual as a tool for administration and was able to extend it into business. This implies that business institutions were substituted for ritual early on in Europe but not in China. It was the entry of the West into China from the mid- to late-nineteenth up to the twentieth century which only very gradually led China to attempt to rest business on law rather than on ritual.

A surviving contract, examined by Faure (2007), signed in 1632 by the four branches of a lineage which contributed to the creation of a lineage trust, was explicitly aimed to be used "to put out capital to seek a profit". Contract culture, which had solidified by the fourteenth century, played an important role in structuring early Chinese businesses (Hansen 1995). Participants in the contracts did not do it as individuals, but as lineages, that is, groups of people tracing common descent rather than the lines of descent themselves. The relationships in the lineage group were regulated more by ritual and patronage than by law. This explains why ritual and patronage played a major role in Chinese business institutions. Ruskola (2000) maintains that, in imperial China, family rules performed many of the functions that American corporation law performs today. He outlines the historical development of Chinese professionally managed commercial enterprises organized in the form of the family and illustrates how these lineage corporations engaged in creative contracting to construct business entities that formally corresponded to the Confucian patrilineal kinships.

To clarify the meaning of the '*corporation*' in imperial China we need to recall the discoveries of modern social historians of China. The respect for ancestors was essential to make people behave. An initial form of shareholding in China came about through ancestor worship (Faure 2007; see also Fei 1992). Land was owned by trusts which provided for sacrifice for ancestors, and the income from the land would be used for the continuity of sacrifice. The trust was a property of the ancestor for whose sacrifice it would have been created. The rules of worship defined the corporation and replaced rules that might govern the management of equity. The lineage organization was created when a 'founding ancestor' had been identified, and showed a lot a flexibility in (re)defining the criteria of membership (Rowe 2009). Ancestor or lineage trusts lasted much longer than business partnerships. Therefore, the ancestor in the name of whom the property was held took on the character of a legal person. The property was held by the corporate group and not by any individual. Members of the trust corresponded to a subgroup of the lineage, and investors bought and sold shares in the trust.

Greif and Tabellini (2010, 2017) have modelled how China and Europe have sustained cooperation in divergent ways, relying on informal enforcement and moral obligations within a group in the former, and on formal enforcement and general moral obligations towards society at large in the latter. However, Greif and Tabellini (2017) may have pushed too far the implications of the contrast between the two social organizations that they associate with pre-modern China and Europe: the lineage and the corporation respectively. They contrast the Chinese lineage, as an organization based on kinship, with the European corporation. The lineage consists of families with common descent, which share reciprocal loyalty and obligations to each other, while the corporation is portrayed as a voluntary association between unrelated individuals established to pursue common interest. In their view the two types of organizations perform similar functions, such as enforcing cooperation among members, providing local public goods, and coordinating interactions with the market or the state. But these organizations are built on very different criteria and operate in a very distinct way. The enforcement of cooperation is based on both reciprocal obligations and personal interactions within a lineage, while it relies on impersonal enforcement procedures within a corporation. Greif and Tabellini (2017) seem to have overlooked that the kinship-based organization, typical of imperial China, did not, as a matter of principle, prevent the emergence of shareholding enterprises.

The pooling of resources along kinship lines in China was not merely a matter of trust, but also reflected a multi-layered sense of common ownership that would play an important role in the development of shareholding institutions. Initially the major asset held by lineage trusts was land, but by the Qing period (1644–1911) many lineage trusts invested their landed wealth in trade, manufacturing and partnership shares. "As templates for the creation of shareholding corporations and as potential tools for wealth available for investment, trusts were a critical component in the cultural construction of the Chinese business entity" (Zelin 2009). Without bank credit, lineage trusts became a privileged means of capital mobilization to finance large-scale investments (Rowe 2009).

In imperial China, different forms of partnership permitted entrepreneurs to put together investment capital and to reinvest the profits in ways which look unexpectedly similar to what joint stock companies made possible in Europe (Pomeranz 1997). The Central government in imperial China prioritized agriculture. Market financing for industrial or commercial ventures was not its concern. Some isolated cases (Zelin 2009) show that entrepreneurs sometimes were still able to use corporate-like structures and securities-trading to finance enterprise. Thus, a capital market for shares, with features of modern share capitalism, emerged in salt mining operations in Zigong in Sichuan province during the Qing dynasty (Zelin 2005; Ho 1954), in an agricultural company in Shandong (Pomeranz 1997), and in coal mines around Beijing (Rowe 2009), in the eighteenth century.

In the case of the Zigong salt yard, there was a notable evolution of shareholding forms which adapted to the changing requirement of business. Initially shares were designed as limited-tenure leases, so that the property of the firm would revert to the owner of the land after some years. The investors in those shares viewed their investments as providing them with the physical right on part of the salt output of the enterprise. With the rise in the technical and capital requirements of the enterprise, the shareholders came to see themselves as participating jointly in a common enterprise, where their interests took the form of dividends and their supervision activity was restricted to meetings of shareholders. Other examples of business partnerships were frequent in Sichuan in the burgeoning coal and iron industries (Zelin 2009).

It is important to emphasize that the salt-extraction arrangements took place under quite unique circumstances, which may limit their general character. First, the monopoly privileges enjoyed by salt merchants implied that their firms would appear exceptionally safe and stable, making them unusually attractive for long-term investment. By contrast, the agricultural product firm examined by Pomeranz (1997), the Yutang company of Jining, which specialized in foodstuffs, especially pickled vegetables and soy sauce, had no special privileges. However, the official position held by the members of the lineage provided indispensable protection. Second, in the salt trade, institutions such as lineage trusts were able to compel the members of an extended family to allow most of the firm's earnings to be re-invested rather than paid out as dividends. In this way, they reproduced the advantages of a joint stock company for long-term accumulation, with a major difference, since stocks could not be sold or transferred outside the household. Such an institutional arrangement was only useful for mobilizing and increasing the capital of a group of extended kin, and only to the extent that potential investors could be reasonably sure they would not need to liquidate their holdings any time soon.

Overall, the differences between China and Europe in terms of financial development would seem to have been a question of scale and widespread application rather than the product of fundamental constraints (Goetzman 2016).

2.2.2 Early Financial Markets

In late fifteenth century Ming China, a market for salt futures arose from the need of the emperor to have grain transported to the troops that garrisoned the northern border. He was able to do so only by mortgaging his monopoly on the production and transport of salt (Faure 2006). The Ming salt certificate was thus known as the grain-salt exchange. Along the eastern coast of China, men from saltern households toiled in the salt fields, producing salt for the government salt monopoly (Puk 2016). The Ming government divided the entire country into salt production and consumption areas; designated consumption areas were supposed to consume salt from particular production areas. The government monopolized salt production and supervised salt consumption. In what turned out to be a sophisticated form of financial engineering, the merchant who intended to deal with salt would first have to transport an agreed quantity of grain to the garrisons in the north. In exchange for that delivery of grain the same merchant would then receive from the government a receipt which he would later be able to exchange in the east (typically Nanjing) for a certificate bearing his entitlement of salt. In essence this grain-salt exchange was a promise the Ming government made to merchants in return for their service in providing grain to soldiers at the borders. The salt certificate therefore was a debt of grain, denominated in salt, owed by the government to merchants. The salt certificate was the closest evidence of public credit in early modern China (Puk 2016).

Once created, the salt certificates very quickly deviated from the path the state had planned for them. Merchants readily found the salt certificate more convenient and valuable than real salt, leading them to abstain from redeeming the salt certificate for salt. In the fifteenth century a speculative market for the salt certificates emerged and, in the sixteenth century, the use of silver fuelled that speculation further. In the early seventeenth century this phenomenon attracted a group of powerful financiers, mostly from Huizhou. Regarding the speculation as an undesirable outcome of the salt-certificate scheme, the Ming government awarded the financiers a hereditary franchise in the salt trade, while imposing on them a hereditary obligation to pay a salt-certificate tax. This 'syndicate system', established in 1617, effectively terminated the speculation in salt certificates, but, at the same time and throughout most of the Qing dynasty, implied that the salt certificate was no longer a form of public debt, but a tax receipt (Puk 2016). In other words, when the Ming emperor abolished the salt certificates, repurchasing them at a fraction of their market value, "by a single stroke of the imperial brush" (Faure 2006) he destroyed a business tradition, making the later emergence of financial instruments in China more difficult. The salt certificate represented a debt that the government was obliged to honour, so what the emperor did was abolish the national debt. From that time onwards the right to trade in salt was granted as an act of imperial patronage.

2.3   Phoenix-like Markets

2.3.1   Stock Market

China's first stock market arose after the mid-1860s (some two centuries after England (Murphy 2009) and the US (Geisst 1997)), at the very start of early industrialization attempts in China. The need was felt to raise funds for modernization, both for domestic and foreign firms. Due to the continuing and worsening pressure to pay for the conduct of war, and war indemnities, which were still bearable from the 1840s to the 1880s (with tens of millions of taels (Gernet 1996)) but became enormous after the defeat against Japan (1895 Shimonozeki treaty) and the Boxer rebellion (reaching hundreds of million taels), the government faced limits to its attempt to provide finance to modern projects. Public-owned ordnance and shipbuilding industries faced funding constraints, due to their exclusive financing by customs duties and indirect tax receipts increasingly absorbed by the indemnities (and the associated debt, Goetzman et al. 2007), within a context of relatively low taxation by the imperial regime (Rowe 2009). The 'government-regulated and merchant managed' scheme from the 1870s (see Sect. 2.5) was an attempt to side-step this constraint (Feuerwerker 1958).

In the 1860s foreigners in the international concessions in Shanghai would meet in tea houses (like coffee houses in Wall Street centuries before) to trade shares, a tradition which would last almost until the end of the nineteenth century. There was no proper listing, but daily share prices were published in the press, typically the *North China Herald*.

This first market was segmented between a few domestic and many foreign firms in the listing process, as well as between a few domestic and many foreign investors—features which would be echoed (in reverse) in modern China's stock market. The foreign-oriented character of the first Shanghai stock market was such that the first formal exchange (the Shanghai Share Broker Association) was not only founded by foreigners, in 1891, but was also restricted to the exclusive trading of foreign stocks. The trading of domestic shares would only take place outside the formal exchange, with only a small number of listed firms (less than 40 by 1911), and would be accessible only to investors located in the vicinity of Shanghai. In a similar way there were very few listed domestic firms in the Chinese modern stock market in the early 1990s.

Domination by banks and insurance companies, followed by shipping-related ones and utilities, with a very minor role of industrial ones, was another dominant feature of the late Qing market. The first industrial companies produced steam ships (from 1868) and weapons (even earlier) and were only listed later (like the Jiangnan arsenal in 1872). From the start, the government or foreigners were involved. There was no security law until the interwar period, and these regulations faced enforcement problems (Cheng and Zhu 2006).

This early stock market either anticipated, or helps better understand, the sometimes surprising, features of the modern stock market in China. Indeed, some of these features echo those of the early market while others take precisely the polar opposite, with the benefit of hindsight, compared to the early unfortunate experience.

2.3.2 Bond Market

The government bond market in China was used in a much more active way than the stock market during the 1860–1949 period. While foreign bonds had been issued already from the 1860s for war financing, the first issuance of domestic bonds only took place in 1894–1895, to finance the war against Japan, since foreign financing had tapered off. The subsequent war indemnities were also financed by bond issuance. During the 1914–1949 period, the government extensively issued domestic bonds, and faced problems due to too large an issuance.

The Qing dynasty in 1860 started to issue sovereign bonds either to fund some activities and companies or to pay war indemnities to the British and French, in both cases with tax receipts or other collaterals. There was no corporate bond market as such. Sovereign debt issuance was used at a low scale and from the very end of the nineteenth century only to finance infrastructure investment such as railway and telegraph construction. This was a timid version of the well-known tsarist Russia example.

The domestic bonds issued in 1894–1895 were misunderstood by local people as another tax since subscription was compulsory. Again, in 1898, for military expenses, the government issued compulsory domestic bonds because foreign debt issue was not available, and a bank run was triggered to try and escape the quasi-tax. At the very end of its reign, the Qing empire issued a "loving the country bond", but the dynasty collapsed before the issuing process was over. In the early 1980s when the PRC restarted issuing government bonds, subscription was similarly compulsory, but this lasted longer, almost a decade, and only later did subscription become voluntary.

At the beginning of the republic in Nanjing, in 1914 and 1915, domestic debt had a good reputation, even though the authorities[1] used the proceeds of the bonds to pay wages of public servants. Then in 1916 the Beijing government issued not only domestic but also foreign debt, and soon enough faced problems because of too large an issuance, direct financing by banks, and its budget deficits preventing it from servicing the debt. Another lesson was drawn by the PRC from that experience.

2.4   The Rebirth of the Phoenix

History repeated itself but in a different form. The PRC initially issued bonds to finance modernization while the late Qing dynasty first did it in 1861 to finance war. The decisive impetus to economic liberalization in the PRC was given in the Plenum of December 1978 which asserted economic modernization as the main objective, emphasizing opening and reform as the fundamental policies, and starting rural reform with the household responsibility system. Once again, the Chinese government, like its predecessor a century earlier, found itself constrained by the limited availability of funds through taxes. So, in the first resort, it repeatedly tapped the bond market, but with limited success. Indeed, the purchase of bonds was compulsory for work units (dispatched among employees), amounting to heavy tax, at least the equivalent of one-month salary in July 1981. While they would eventually be repaid after a decade, such bonds were not transferable. In 1980–1985 their issuance represented 25 billion

[1] After 1920, the bond market helped the government to solve its financing problems (Zhu 2006).

Chinese renminbi (RMB). Then a rising series of issues culminated with 22 billion in the single year of 1989. A secondary interbank market for government bonds was set up in 1988, and later extended to 28 and then 55 cities.

There was an attempt to issue corporate bonds (so-called enterprise bonds) from 1986 onwards, beginning at a modest scale, close to 10 billion, rising to almost 50 billion RMB in 1992, but with no secondary market. Subsequently this market vanished because the corporate bonds were not paid back, making them a little bit similar to shares or non-performing loans. This illustrates the blurred border between loans, shares and bonds in the early reformed PRC setting.

The financing of the enterprise reform in the 1980s relied on a sequential strategy. The first component was the creation of a banking system, with the externalization of commercial banking out of the People's Bank of China (PBoC) into four newly created State-Owned Banks (SOBs), that is, Industrial and Commercial Bank of China (ICBC), China Construction Bank (CCB), Agricultural Bank of China (ABC), and Bank of China (BoC). These new banks were assigned the financing of SOEs, which would relieve the government budget from this financing via subsidies. Such an origin would leave a long legacy. Indeed, bank loans, to a large extent, kept the character of subsidies, in as much as they would turn into apparent non-performing loans (NPLs). Banks loans were like perpetuities.

The blurred distinction between bonds, bank loans, and shares was thus inherited from the previous dominance of subsidies. The initial nationalization by the PRC of all economic enterprises and financial institutions then unified all these activities under one roof with a single source of financing, which was the government budget. To some extent to fully get rid of such a system would be a persistent worry for the authorities over the subsequent six decades.

This context helps understand the recurring difficulties in providing financing to SOEs. The major reforms of the financial system, initiated in 1984–1985, complemented the landmark reforms of SOEs in two steps: first, stimulating the development of collective and small enterprises and then selecting three pilot cities (Beijing, Shanghai, Guangzhou) to experiment the shareholding system. In the second half of 1984 a few SOEs started to issue shares as unregulated private placements. *Feile* Audio and *Yanzhong* industries were the first two companies to issue shares in Shanghai in September 1984, underwritten by financial intermediaries (the *Jingnan* district branch of the Shanghai Trust and Investment Company (TIC), subsidiary of ICBC). Over-the-counter trading (OTC) of these shares started two years later at the desks of the Shanghai TIC. One-sided trading was typical of this early market, with only buying orders.

Overall the re-emergence of share issuance and trading was active, rather spontaneous and somewhat hectic. It initially corresponded with the decentralized nature of industrial expansion, in the form of a shareholding cooperative system based on unregulated private placements. After 1978 the priority was put on financing rural TVEs with Rural Credit Cooperatives (RCC), followed by their urban counterparts Urban Credit Cooperatives (UCC) associated with urban and enterprise reforms (Girardin 1997). The landmark industrial reforms of the mid-1980s gave a decisive impetus to the restructuring of some enterprises into shareholding companies, largely initiated by the Shenzhen local government.

After 1986 the shareholding system reached the large SOEs, which started to issue shares in a public or semi-public way, leading to the emergence of a secondary market (following the 'Shenzhen Provisions', Walter and Howie 2001). In this 'coupon-clipping' experience shares were akin to corporate bonds. They carried a fixed dividend and had a maturity (2–4 years) at which the principal would be paid back. But there was no investment bank to underwrite such quasi-bonds. The firms would themselves issue bonds bought by their employees or locally by households. Before September 1986 trading was informal, but, from then on, the Shanghai TIC started OTC trading. In September 1987 the first security company was set up in Shenzhen. In 1988 the PBoC provided initial capital and approved the establishment of 33 security companies across the country. All these security companies were strongly connected with the four SOBs.

In March 1990 the central government allowed Shanghai and Shenzhen to start the listing of companies. 'Temporary regulations for share issue and trading' were released, for Shanghai in November 1990 and for Shenzhen in May 1991. This led to a quick response by Shanghai, which officially opened its exchange in December 1990, followed unofficially by Shenzhen the following day, only officialized in June 1991. Shenzhen already announced the composition of its index on April 4, 1991 (with a basis of 100 on April 3, 1990). Shanghai actually did it only more than three months later, on July 15, 1991 (with a basis of 100 on December 19, 1990). In January 1992 the Shenzhen government issued 'Temporary Regulations on Shareholding Companies'. Thus, the competition between the two cities was very intense form the very start of the modern Chinese stock market. This beginning was very slow since by 1990 there were only 8 listed shares in Shanghai and 6 in Shenzhen.

Overall the second half of the 1980s looked only as a sort of training period or warming up. There was no regulated and organized stock exchange but only OTC transactions (Walter and Howie 2001). The setting up of shareholding companies had resulted from bottom-up initiatives in Shanghai and Shenzhen. Locally-based initiatives were indeed allowed as experiments within the newly set up Special Economic Zones (SEZs). The associated unregulated share markets were incomplete and highly speculative, built on decentralized developments.

2.5   LESSONS FROM CHINA'S HISTORICAL EXPERIENCE

2.5.1   Government Involvement

Initially, in the late Qing period, there was no control, no law and no regulation either for firms or the stock market. Companies were founded either by foreigners or through the 'government-controlled and merchant-managed' (GCMM) scheme.[2] This was a sui generis scheme, called *Guan du shang ban*, introduced under the self-strengthening movement initiated during the Tongzhi restoration (1862–1874), subsequent to the victory over the Taiping rebellion, which only took place in 1864 after upheavals lasting a decade and a half. The GCMM scheme borrowed heavily from the prior organization of the government salt monopoly. As we saw above in a different context, official supervisors were appointed by the government but the rights to extract, transport, and sell salt were either sold or farmed out to merchant groups, which were still active in the late nineteenth century on a regional or provincial basis (Feuerwerker 1958; Puk 2016). This salt organization was a fiscal institution which enjoyed full monopoly rights. The major features of that scheme were transposed into modern-style enterprises set up in the late Qing empire.

In the first major example of the *Guan du shang ban* scheme, the shares of the first Chinese joint-stock company to be listed in 1872, the China

---

[2] Such a scheme operated alongside fully private, fully public enterprises, as well as some firms with joint private and public management (Feuerwerker 1958). The classification of company ownership and management in the late Qing dynasty sounds quite similar to what the reformed PRC would enforce.

Merchant's Steamship Navigation Company, were subscribed by local merchants who also managed the firm, while the government gave the impetus and provided an initial loan which turned out to be perpetual (Yang 2006). The interconnection between businessmen and government officials was quite strong. This combined western company organization with Chinese specific dominance of government officials. These companies, which served the government, even though they were listed, had a semi-official status, with no report of their own but only official records (Feuerwerker 1958), and their manager, though a private merchant, also held an official rank.

After 1911, the government was also heavily involved in another way. Companies only rarely issued shares and the main trading activity in secondary markets took place for local government bonds. The number of listed companies was unchanged in 1930 compared to 1910, and this number was even lower than 100 both in 1920 and in 1940.

In 1914 the new Republic of China issued the Security Exchange Law. An exchange called the Shanghai Stock Market Association was then opened, with a little more than ten members, trading 20 stocks, bonds, and some commodities. Each of the two governments ruling China at the time set up their own exchange. In 1916, in Shanghai, Sun Yat-sen created the Shanghai Stocks and Commodities Exchange and tried to fund his government by issuing bonds. The government of Yuan Shikai in North China set up its own Beijing Stock Exchange. In 1920 the Shanghai market was the only one to remain. Even Chiang Kai-shek was involved in stock trading. He was a successful stock broker who later became political leader.

In the late 1910s more than 70 exchanges were set up in Shanghai, among them 38 in one month. In the interwar period there were many regional exchanges. A Security Exchange Law was issued by the nationalist government in 1929, as well as a Company Law. In 1939 the Beijing market was closed due to lack of trading, and the old Shanghai stock market was closed due to the war with Japan. The Japanese occupying forces decreed the opening in Shanghai of a new exchange, in September 1943, called the Chinese Commercial Security Exchange, with 85 companies listed, and only with spot trading. They tried to set up other exchanges in Beijing and Tianjin, but these attempts were not successful because volatility was too high with discontinuous trading due to hostilities.

After its victory, the national government closed the Japanese stock exchange in Shanghai, and in September 1946 set up a new Shanghai

Stock Exchange, the phoenix's rebirth, where 199 companies were traded. There was a short boom in 1947, followed by a collapse. In 1948, during the hyperinflation, the stock market became very hectic. The PRC closed that market after the fall of Shanghai in May 1949, to temporarily open markets in Beijing and Shanghai, to be followed by a nearly four-decade-long interruption from 1952 onwards.

The government was involved in the domestic stock market in a hands-off or hands-on way from its foundation in the 1870s until the 1920s. Early in the twentieth century, the government was able to transplant the foreign laws on paper (such as the company Law of 1904). There was then a quite rich and complete set of regulations, but actual enforcement was very poor. The authorities could set up supervisory institutions which played a dominant role in the market. The government never set up an effective information disclosure system. It always wanted to directly control the market instead of providing a level-playing field. The very powerful government, hardly able to enforce regulations, faced fake information disclosure by companies, which distorted the market.

The listed companies in the late Qing dynasty not only had to report to the government, but also had to pay a so-called official dividend, alongside the standard one. Chinese listed companies' shareholders' meetings had no function. Only the officials connected with the company played a governing role.

2.5.2 Speculative Market Crashes

The early market was characterized from the start by recurrent speculative episodes with expanding magnitude (1866, 1872, 1883) and three major crashes (1883, 1910, and 1921) (Zhu 1998) during the first 70 years (Fig. 2.1). These upheavals reflect the fact that foreigners had a strong influence and interference in the market, imprinting it a speculative character.

In the 1870s, investors were new to the market and rather unable to distinguish profitable from non-profitable companies. All kinds of funds poured in, and the major money houses began to provide loans for leverage to enterprises and individuals. A stock fever in 1882 brought a rise in many stocks, by more than 100% (Chen 2006), followed by a 70% fall from September the following year (Fig. 2.1). The 1883 crisis was mainly foreign, but had a domestic source linked to a business failure in the silk industry. In 1883, Xueyan Hu, the richest man in China at that time,

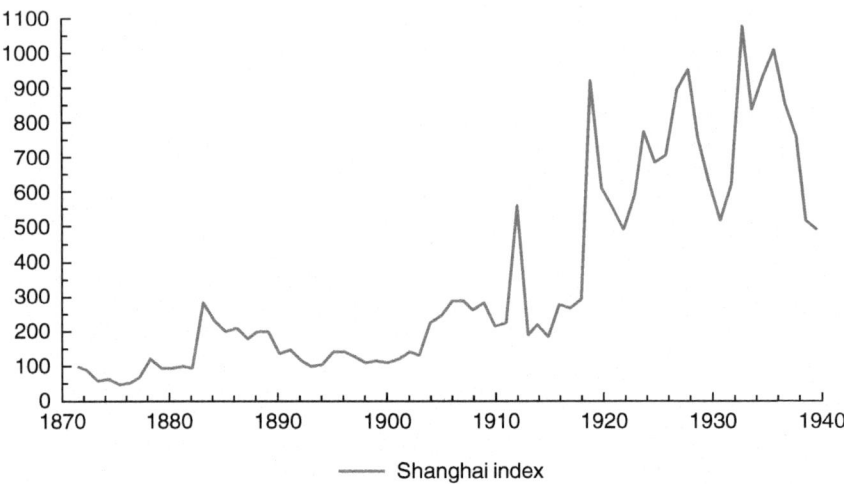

Fig. 2.1 Shanghai's first stock market in historical perspective: 1870–1940. Shanghai stock (value-weighted) index in U.S. dollar (1871 = 100). Source: Goetzman et al. (2007)

seeing the profit opportunities of silk-weaving enterprises in China, decided to monopolize the silk. However, just after he had spent huge sums of money to acquire all the raw silk in the country, thus raising the price, Brazil suddenly announced a record harvest of silk. As a result, the price of Chinese raw silk started plummeting. Hu went bankrupt and many local listed silk-weaving enterprises closed down. The impact of this 'silk war' had far-reaching consequences, leading to the collapse of some money houses and the first stock market crash in Chinese history.

The early twentieth century speculative wave is another interesting case. Speculation started from a foreign concern: Malaysian rubber (Thomas 2001). A fake venture was set up in 1903 by a rogue British businessman. The price of rubber skyrocketed, driving the share prices of rubber companies to the sky (from an initial level of 60 to more than 1450 for the Shanghai Rubber Company), and then, when the price of rubber collapsed, due to demand restrictions in the US, the corresponding share prices fell by 50–70%. The company managers went back to the UK, with a disastrous impact on the image of the stock market. More importantly for China, high-ranking officials were also involved, who went as far as using tax receipts to try and beef up the market. Government finances, already in an appalling state due to war indemnities, were even further deteriorated. Foreign pressure was also widespread, as testified by the timid attempt at financing—by domestic share issuance— the budding domestic railway industry which was thwarted by the late Qing government. The latter chose to nationalize that railway, and opted for the use of foreign loans, a move which was one of the immediate causes of the overthrow of the dynasty in 1911, associated with the railway rights recovery movement (Goetzman 2016).

In the early 1920s, Trust companies increasingly attracted funds from both individuals and institutions, and started manipulating some stocks, amplifying a fever wave. Native banks were lending on margin on a massive scale, feeding a bubble (Chen 2006). When they started making margin calls late 1921, prices fell sharply, triggering the failure of banks and trust companies. The 1921 crash damped investors' appetite for shares for decades (Zhu 2006), the stock market in Shanghai was persistently bearish, and the public debt market replaced it. This situation continued until 1938, when the government debt market plummeted due to the outbreak of the anti-Japanese war. However, the stock market quietly recovered and prospered rapidly in the Shanghai concession. There was no unified regulated market,[3] and securities were freely bought and sold by securities firms. At the same time, there were very different prices for the same stock, and over-the-counter transactions as well as parallel market transactions were very active. Stock prices skyrocketed; some of them even exceeded ten times their issuing value. The exchange was often forced to stop trading due to excessive price fluctuations. In the last year of the anti-Japanese War of Resistance, the stock exchange became very speculative, with bubbles which readily burst. By the end of 1945, these stock certificates formed a pile of waste paper.

In this light, one may understand better why the PRC was reluctant to recreate a stock market, and, when it did so after the 1978 reforms, it chose the polar opposite of the first Shanghai market, allowing only the participation of domestic firms and domestic investors. Unfortunately, the authorities may not have been careful enough to avoid the speculative aspect.

Dividend distribution in the early market, during the late nineteenth century, had no direct relationship with earnings and was maintained, even in the absence of sufficient earnings, with numbers like 12 or 8.

---

[3] During the 1937–1939 period, the market was very incomplete and speculative with heavy government intervention (Bai 2000).

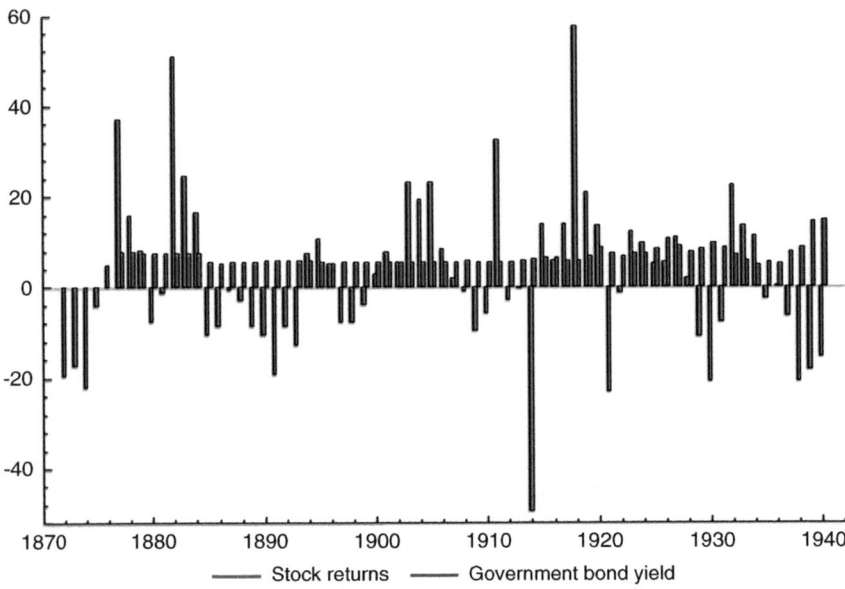

Fig. 2.2 Shanghai Stock returns and Chinese government bond yields, in dollars: 1871–1940. Source: Bond yields: Global Financial data; Shanghai annual dividend-inclusive stock returns in dollar, computed with Goetzman et al.'s (2007) data

Shares were treated somewhat like fixed income products. Dividend yields were dwarfed by exchange rate movements. As shown in Fig. 2.2, from 1877 to 1940 the average yearly excess (dividend inclusive) return was sizeable in domestic currency (3.5%), helped by a small dividend yield (2.07%), but depressed by a high bond yield (6.86%). However, such excess returns were negative in dollar terms (−1.35%), due to sizable domestic currency depreciation (4.94%) with large volatility.

2.6   SUMMARY AND CONCLUSIONS

Based on kinship, the early Chinese lineage trusts creatively used contracts and rules to establish a Confucian patrilineal business entity. Some early companies used this setting to operate in some regions.

China's first stock market appeared in the concession of Shanghai in the mid-1860s. This foreign-dominated market was highly speculative, as evidenced by the major crashes that followed in the next 50 years. After the establishment of the Republic of China, especially between 1916 and 1919, there were many stock markets across the country. But after the 1921 stock market crash, only the Shanghai stock market was left. In the interwar period, although stock trading was bleak, bond trading was active due to issuance by the government of a large number of bonds, attracting investors with high yields.

Although the Japanese established the Shanghai stock market in 1943, during their occupation of Shanghai, it involved only spot transactions, was small in scale and had a short life. At the beginning of 1946, the National government set up a stock market in Shanghai. Although it was quite active, this market quickly collapsed, due to civil war and hyperinflation. In 1949, with the creation of the PRC, this market was shut down, markets temporarily opened in Beijing and Tianjin but an almost 40-year interruption began in 1952.

After three decades in the PRC, with economic reforms that began in December 1978, the government issued bonds several times, but no true market was active due to forced buying. The enterprise reform, begun in 1984, gave birth to a complex ownership structure with unique Chinese characteristics. In many large cities, there were active, spontaneous, and unregulated stock transactions. In early 1990, the central government banned stock transactions in most major cities, and only allowed stock exchanges in Shanghai and Shenzhen.

Throughout its Phoenix-like history, the Chinese stock market has been dominated either by foreigners, or by the government, and repeatedly closed and reopened. It is no wonder that Deng Xiaoping later said that China can try the stock market, and if it does not work, it will be closed off.

The early Chinese stock market in the late Qing dynasty, dominated by foreigners, was not supervised and lacked a formal listing process, and speculation was dominant. The subsequent republican securities market also experienced recurrent waves of speculation and collapses. The modern Chinese stock market after 1990 again experienced excessive speculation. Speculation thus appears as an inherent feature of the Chinese stock market.

References

Bai, L. 2000. Historical Study of Shanghai Stock Market 1937–49. *Nankai University Journal* 4: 49–55.

Chen, Z. 2006. Stock Market in China's Modernization Process: Its Past, Present and Future Prospects. Working Paper, Yale School of Management.

Cheng, J., and W. Zhu. 2006. China Stock Market Involution: 1873–1949. *Economics Research Journal* 12: 114–123.

Faure, D. 2006. *China and Capitalism: A History of Business Enterprise in Modern China.* Hong Kong: Hong Kong University Press.

———. 2007. *Emperor and Ancestor: State and Lineage in South China.* Stanford, CA: Stanford University Press.

Fei, X. 1992. *From the Soil: The Foundations of Chinese Society.* University of California Press.

Feuerwerker, A. 1958. *China's Early Industrialization: Sheng Hsuan-Huai (1844–1916) and Mandarin Enterprise.* Cambridge, MA: Harvard University Press.

Geisst, C.R. 1997. *Wall Street: A History.* Oxford: Oxford University Press.

Gernet, J. 1996. *A History of Chinese Civilization.* Cambridge: Cambridge University Press.

Girardin, E. 1997. *Banking Sector Reform and Credit Control in China.* Paris: Development Centre Studies, OECD Development Centre.

Goetzman, W.N. 2016. *Money Changes Everything: How Finance Made Civilization Possible.* Princeton, NJ: Princeton University Press.

Goetzman, W., A. Ukhov, and N. Zhu. 2007. China and the World Financial Markets: Modern Lessons from Historical Globalization. *Economic History Review* 60 (2): 267–312.

Greif, A., and G. Tabellini. 2010. Cultural and Institutional Bifurcation: China and Europe Compared. *American Economic Review, Papers and Proceedings* 100 (2): 135–140.

———. 2017. The Clan and the Corporation: Sustaining Cooperation in China and Europe. *Journal of Comparative Economics* 45 (1): 1–35.

Hansen, V. 1995. *Negotiating Daily Life in Traditional China: How Ordinary People Used Contracts, 600–1400.* New Haven, CT: Yale University Press.

Ho, P. 1954. The Salt Merchants of Yang-Chou: A Study of Commercial Capitalism in Eighteenth-Century China. *Harvard Journal of Asiatic Studies* 17 (1/2): 130–168.

Murphy, A.L. 2009. *The Origins of English Financial Markets: Investment and Speculation before the South Sea Bubble.* Cambridge: Cambridge University Press.

Pomeranz, K. 1997. "Traditional" Chinese Business Forms Revisited: Family, Firm, and Financing in the History of the Yutang Company of Jining, 1779–1956. *Late Imperial China* 18: 1–38.

Puk, W.-K. 2016. *The Rise and Fall of a Public Debt Market in 16th-Century China: The Story of the Ming Salt Certificate.* Leiden: Brill.

Rowe, W.T. 2009. *China's Last Empire: The Great Qing.* Cambridge, MA: Harvard University Press.

Ruskola, T. 2000. Conceptualizing Corporations and Kinship: Comparative Law and Development Theory in a Chinese Perspective. *Stanford Law Review* 52: 1599–1729.

Thomas, A.W. 2001. *Western Capitalism in China: A History of the Shanghai Stock Exchange*. Aldershot: Ashgate.

Walter, C.A., and F.J.T. Howie. 2001. *To Get Rich is Glorious': China's Stock Markets in the '80s and '90s*. Basingstoke: Palgrave.

Yang, Z. 2006. *Corporations and Corporate Governance in Late Qing*. Beijing: Commercial Press.

Zelin, M. 2005. *The Merchants of Zigong: Industrial Entrepreneurship in Early Modern China*. New York: Columbia University Press.

———. 2009. The Firm in Early Modern China. *Journal of Economic Behaviour and Organization* 71: 623–637.

Zhu, Y. 1998. Three Stock Market Upsurge in Modern Shanghai Securities Market. *China Economic History Studies* 3: 58–70.

———. 2006. China Securities Markets: 1918–1937. *Fudan University Journal* 2: 74–85.

CHAPTER 3

A Government-Dominated Financial System

Abstract The design and development of a financial system with Chinese characteristics have been dominated by the government since the 1980s. The creation of the stock market is only one stage in that process. Three major features of such government domination are emphasized in this chapter.

First, we will review the difficulties raised when trying to fit a stock market into a socialist market economy. We will consider the motivations behind the transformation in the channels of financing of the economy. While the initial move, in the mid-1980s, involved a shift of the financing of state-owned enterprises from government subsidies to bank-intermediated financing, the subsequent move, in the early 1990s, marked a partial shift to direct financing, with the creation of the stock market.

Second, we will present the major stages of development of the stock market, including the crucial step of Chinese-style privatization, involving the privatization of small- and medium-sized SOEs, sometimes with insider privatization, and the listing of large SOEs, leading much later to the split-share reform bringing the float closer to capitalization.

Third, the heavy involvement of the government is strongly felt in new market creation, the creation and control of institutional investors and intermediaries, as well as the design and monitoring of the functioning of the market. External financial liberalization has been only very limited and gradual, relying on tightly controlled idiosyncratic schemes.

© The Author(s) 2019   33
E. Girardin, Z. Liu, *Demystifying China's Stock Market*,
https://doi.org/10.1007/978-3-030-17123-0_3

Keywords Government domination • Reform • Socialist market economy • Chinese characteristics • Ownership

3.1   INTRODUCTION

The dominance of the government has been the driving force of the design and development of a financial system with Chinese characteristics, and the creation of the stock market can only be understood as one of the stages in the creation and development of that financial system. The transformations in the channels of financing of the economy played a key role in this development. Firms' financing stopped relying exclusively on government subsidies to state-owned enterprises (SOEs), and came to rely on loans granted by the newly created four state owned banks (SOBs). Bank deposits, that is, household savings, thus became the privileged source of firms' external finance. The creation of the stock market in the early 1990s marked a partial shift from such indirect financing to direct financing. At the same time the listing of banks enabled them to shift the burden of non-performing loans (NPLs) to a new source of financing.

The institutional approach (a la Acemoglu 2013) views China's increasingly effective economic institutions as doomed to reach rising limits due to 'unsuited' political institutions. This chapter will rather argue that it is artificial in the case of China to separate the two types of institutions. Indeed "China is a significant counterexample to the existing literature on law, institutions, finance and growth" (Allen et al. 2005).

This chapter will first spell out the major challenge met by the authorities when they tried to fit the genie of the stock market inside the bottle of the socialist market economy. We will then discuss the major motivations and preconditions for the shift to direct financing from the previous indirect financing via bank loans. Then we will consider the subsequent stages of development of the market from the mid-1990s to the new millennium, with the privatization of small- and medium-sized SOEs, while keeping large ones under state ownership with gradual listing, the split-share reform, and the opening and deepening of the market. Third, we will emphasize the dominant role played in the market by the regulator, acting as the operational arm of the government for the creation of new markets, the setting up and control of new institutional investors, as well as the day-to-day management of the market and problem solving.

3.2   The Conundrum: How to Fit the Genie of the Stock Market Inside the Bottle of the Socialist Market Economy?

Features of China's stock market, which can be at first sight surprising for academics and practitioners familiar with stock markets in OECD (Organization for Economic Cooperation and Development) countries, can be rationalized both by the organizational challenges faced by the reformers of China's financial system, and by the operational context of the early 1990s. At the organizational level, China's stock markets have confronted its creators with a catch-22 situation whose origin can be traced back to the lack of a template for inserting a stock market in a socialist market economy. At an operational level, the myriad of share types which arose at the very time of the creation of the modern stock market can only be understood in the context of accounting[1] practices which still pertained to the logic of a planned economy.

In the wake of Deng Xiaoping's early 1992 'Southern Tour', the 14th Party Congress clearly targeted the creation of a socialist market economy. However, as very recently emphasized by Perkins (2019) in his attempt to assess the progress in China's economic reforms, this landmark Party Congress refrained from providing a comprehensive definition of what this would imply. With the perspective of two-and-a-half decades, the target seems to have been to create a market system emulating that of high-income countries but mixed with very substantial state ownership of enterprises and a leading role for the state. Still, this does not in any way tell us how the stock market was supposed to fit into the picture.

The difficulty met by the reformers in China in the late 1980s was the lack of prior thinking about the place the financial system should occupy in the functioning of a socialist market economy. The literature from the first half of the twentieth century (a la Lange and Taylor 1938), which endeavoured to spell out the way in which a socialist market economy would work, simply did not consider that a stock market would be part of

---

[1] Accounting in the history of China may have used the double-entry form as early as the late fifteenth century (Lin 1992). However, this is a subject of controversy (surveyed by Hoskin and Macve 2012).

it (Pistor and Xu 2005; Du and Xu 2005). In the view of these early theoreticians, in a socialist market economy the property-right structure would be dominated by state ownership, with no need of a stock market for the trading of shares in productive assets incorporated in companies. The state would ensure the protection of state property and enforce contracts with its administrative powers, making private property rights all but redundant. To be fair, at the time of Lange and Taylor, there was no conceptualization of the serious incentive problems present in state-owned enterprises, stemming from the analogous disconnect between property rights and control characterizing publicly-traded firms in market economies. Solving these problems could thus not be a concern for this early literature (Du and Xu 2005).

The incentive problems in state-owned enterprises were, however, accounted for in the 1980s (Kornai 1980), and the role that the stock market could play came to be acknowledged, but only very late, on the very eve of the collapse of the Eastern bloc (Nuti 1989). Hungary even set up a stock market (Jarai 1989), though restricting share trading among enterprises (Nuti 1989).

A vivid debate took place in China after the mid-1980s, opposing the supporters of goods-market price reform, as a way to improve the efficiency of SOEs, personified by Jinglian Wu (2005), and those of ownership reform, represented by Yining Li, a disciple of Kornai (a debate well tracked by Fewsmith 1994).

The designers of the stock market in China could borrow from two alternative paradigms. The paradigm of financial development in an emerging economy (a la McKinnon 1993), recommends a sequencing of financial liberalization and the opening of markets (Harwood and Smith 1997). The late-developers' paradigm (a la Gerschenkron 1962) rather recommends heavy state intervention for backward economies in the process of catching-up, with little place for stock markets (Bowles and White 1993). Within China, each of these alternative views has been in a recurrent way championed by different lobby groups.

Without any prior template, the Chinese reformers of the early 1990s had to invent a new model of a stock market with Chinese characteristics. They could also draw lessons from prior experiences of China with financial markets, which we reviewed in Chap. 2. From the Qing stock market they would depart by designing a market dominated by domestic issuers and investors, in contrast with earlier foreign dominance, but they would borrow the use of capital markets to provide financing to the government and state-controlled firms. From the experience of the 1980s they learned the downside of the half-way house represented by the 'coupon-clipping' experience where shares (bought by the firm's employees or locally by households) were actually akin to corporate bonds, because they carried a fixed dividend and had a maturity at which the principal would be paid back, and were not exchange- but over-the-counter-traded.

It is well-known from finance textbooks, as well as from the practice of high-income countries, that shares should represent, on the demand side, a right of ownership of part of a company and of a variable income for the investor, and on the supply side, an obligation for the company which issues the shares. In early 1990s China, stock markets had to be somehow squeezed into an economy where state planning had not yet vanished and where there was no private ownership. Setting up stock exchanges aimed at improving the operating efficiency of SOEs, while ensuring that the state was still fully controlling them. Within such a framework it seems difficult to say what equities would actually represent (Walter and Howie 2006). They would only provide investors with an opportunity to make capital gains when trading, and possibly to be paid a very occasional dividend. The firms would have no obligation to minority shareholders, only to the state. In China's stock market the state is omnipotent; it operates, regulates, or legislates for the, markets, and cashes-in the funds raised during the listing of firms that it owns.

The design of shares and stock exchanges strongly relied on the principles driving the accounting system prevailing in China in the 1980s. In accordance with the state planning system, accounting was still rules-based and not 'principles' based. It consisted in a "code of extremely specific accounting treatment developed to meet nearly every situation" (Walter et al. 2006: 68). Accordingly, there was no integrated single balance sheet, but three fund categories: a "fixed" fund for fixed investment assets, a "current fund" for working capital and a "special fund", mainly for depreciation allowances, but also for employees' incentives, product development, etc. In every sub-balance sheet, funds in each category were sourced in a different way.

Initially, in the early 1990s, the authorities were faced with the necessity to decide how to allocate share capital according to its source to each of the fixed and current accounts. Depending on what type of asset was contributed, the related shares would be carried in the old fund source location on the three sub-balance sheets of the firm. The basic difference was between fixed assets and cash contributions. The state had ownership on state-owned assets, presumably fixed assets, while individuals, say employees of the firm or outsiders, would own individual shares corresponding to cash contributions, which could be traded (Walter and Howie 2006).

This accounting framework is the foundation of the very specific categorization of share types defined by the benchmark 1992 accounting regulations (known as the 'Standard Opinion'). Ownership of fixed assets would correspond either to State shares, held by state agencies and organizations at the central or local level, or to Legal Person shares held by enterprises, institutions or social group with corresponding status. Cash contributions would correspond either to Individual shares, held by the firm's employees and outside individual investors, or to foreign shares, denominated in foreign currency and held by foreign investors. The firm as such, in the western meaning of the term, did not properly exist. Only the particular assets contributed by each investor had a formal existence. On China's stock market, there was no trading in firms, only in shares (Walter and Howie 2006).

With the benefit of hindsight, the major reforms of the late 1990s and mid 2000s imply that the stock markets may not have been fully consistent with a socialist market economy. In the view of some observers a domination of state ownership in listed firms could possibly turn out to be "a transitory phenomenon in China's economic transition" (Du and Xu, 2005).

3.3   Chinese-Style Privatization

3.3.1   Multidimensional Ownership Reform

With respect to ownership reform,[2] we learnt from the experience of the 1990s in the former Soviet Union and its satellites that the authorities face three series of choices. The first choice is between mass privatization and insider privatization. The former involves the wide distribution of shares to the public, as exemplified in the 1990s with voucher distribution to the public, while the latter gives the opportunity to employees and/or managers to acquire shares in the company in which they work. The second choice is between a big bang and a gradual privatization, implying an implementation either in one go or over time. The third choice concerns the differential treatment of public-owned firms according to their size

---

[2] On the background of privatization in socialist countries, see Roland (2000).

(collectives, small- and medium-sized SOEs, and large SOEs). The geographical dimension added a fourth choice to the process in China, due to the role of deconcentration across three main levels of jurisdiction (province, city, and county) in its economic reforms.

In the 1980s the Chinese authorities did not make any explicit choice. In a decentralized way de facto private ownership arose outside the previous ownership framework, which legally only allowed either state or collective ownership, in the form of the new Township and Village Enterprises (TVEs). The latter formally tried to brand themselves as collectives but were truly private. Before the 1980s, collectives would usually act as subcontractors to SOEs. With the reform, TVEs, newly set up in the countryside (see Naughton 2007), gradually took over this function, benefiting from much lower costs, thanks to their use of labour and land released by the agricultural reform, and smoothly driving the old collectives out of business. In that process the TVEs in some way rebranded themselves as collectives, thus blurring the distinction between private and collective ownership. In other words, the initiative in the ownership reform took place in a decentralized fashion. In an unintended way this process triggered, by a chain reaction, the subsequent ownership reforms, even though the initial process was very fuzzy. There was legally no room for private ownership in the 1980s.

In the second half of the 1980s some collectives started to brand themselves in a blurred way as shareholding companies. A subset of those shareholding companies managed to get listed, first in Shanghai, and then in Shenzhen, very soon followed by a myriad of other cities. This means that the initiative moved up one level in the decentralized structure, from townships to cities. De facto the privatization process for public-sector firms was started at a local level in a hands-off way without any formal decision by the central authorities. This process took place, gradually and rather disorderly, not as a big bang.

The volume of securities issued rose and the number of investors grew, creating a huge demand for securities brokerages and trading. Over-the-counter transactions then appeared for stocks and bonds. In 1986, Shenyang Trust & Investment Corporation (TIC) became the first company to provide brokerage services for stock and bond trading. The Shanghai TIC, a subsidiary of the Industrial and Commercial bank of China (ICBC), was the first to set up secondary trading. In April 1988, the trading of Treasury bonds by retail investors was permitted in seven cities. By the end of that year, such trading had spread across the whole country. This created the earliest form of the secondary bond market in the PRC.

In the late 1980s, the local governments of both Shanghai and Shenzhen were very eager to find funding for the rapid development of local economic growth. This provided them with strong incentives to set up exchanges as soon as this possibility was offered by the central government to large cities. Other cities (such as Chengdu, Guangzhou, Tientsin, etc.) than the happy few had made some unofficial attempts in this direction but had less bargaining power with the central authorities and were thus not as successful in their quest to open a local stock market. The central authorities, in March 1988, closed all 41 unauthorized regional stock exchanges. They had no choice but to decide to legalize only two stock exchanges in Shanghai and Shenzhen.

Initially the exchanges were very narrow. At the end of 1991, the Shanghai Stock Exchange (SSE) had 8 listed stocks and 25 members, while the Shenzhen Stock Exchange (SZSE) had 6 listed stocks and 15 members. On April 4 of 1991, SZSE launched the Shenzhen Composite Index, taking the previous day as the base of 100 points. On July 15, 1991, SSE launched the Shanghai Composite Index, taking December 19, 1990 as its base of 100 points.

As mentioned above, from the start, the creation of the stock market involved a multi-layered shareholding structure, with State-Owned shares, Legal Person shares, Collective and Individual shares. Among those, initially only the individual ones, and later some of the collective or legal person shares, could be traded in the exchange.

Due to their spectacular growth, the TVEs very soon out-competed many small- and medium-sized SOEs located in urban areas, which started to accumulate losses. The authorities were then compelled, in the first half of the 1990s, to decide about the format of ownership reform. The "seize the big and release the small"[3] policy was a consequence of this. With respect to small- and medium-sized SOEs the insider privatization option was taken. Either employees or managers got shares in the company which employed them, on a case-by-case basis. The treatment was also jurisdiction-specific at many levels of deconcentration, leaving each level in charge of reforming the ownership of the firms which it controlled.

---

[3] A review of the content and implications of this policy is carried out by Hsieh and Song (2015).

After 1992 private ownership appeared as a legal possibility. Large SOEs started to face mutual competition due to price and economic liberalization, as well as from large TVEs. Large SOEs had multiple tasks, holding large social responsibilities. The huge share of loss-making SOEs forced the central government leaders to take the ownership reform seriously. Instead of relying on mass privatization in a big-bang way, the central authorities decided to gradually list some selected SOEs with a multiple-share structure, which actually separated the holding of shares from the ownership of firms. Even though this was decided at the central level, very soon the initiative moved to the deconcentrated levels, due to the quota system for IPOs, where local authorities at each level of jurisdiction would compete for the quotas (see Chap. 5).

The success of the advocates of an exclusive price reform, in the second half of the 1980s, was only a short-term victory, since price liberalization, creating competition and leading to losses for SOEs, gradually made it impossible to avoid ownership reform. The Chinese ownership reforms were multidimensional, and not restricted to the simple choice between mass and insider privatization. They included the size of public sector firms, the time frame of reforms and deconcentrated administrative aspects. Over a quarter of a century from 1984 to 2008, China's ownership reform indeed used multiple combinations of the four dimensions of privatization outlined at the beginning of this section.

The multitask character of China's large SOEs has also been a factor delaying their privatization (Bai et al. 2000, 2006). Pre-restructuring, those SOEs had to offer a social safety net to their employees (including healthcare, housing, schooling of their children, pensions, etc.), diverting resources away from the objective of increasing value added, or other economic objectives. This multitask nature shows the inherent limits of an assessment of the efficiency of such firms on the sole basis of their performance, that is, profitability. In the absence of alternative social safety net arrangements, privatization of large SOEs should only be gradual and incomplete. During that phase SOEs had low incentives to divert resources away from their social safety net activities, and thus little incentive to generate profits. SOE managers' employment contracts would take this multitask character into account and assign them non-financial objectives (Bai and Xu 2005). At a later stage, when an alternative social safety net had started to be put in place, or some SOEs had specialized in providing social security, privatization of SOEs could be initiated on a large scale.[4]

[4] For an assessment of the effects of privatization see Bai et al. (2009).

The 'Chinese style' federalism (Montinola et al. 1995) provided a foundation for 'Chinese style' privatization (Cao et al. 1999). In this form of federalism deconcentrated[5] levels of government, that is, the representatives of the central government in the different levels of geographical jurisdictions, were empowered with authority over the economy within their locality. Such local governments faced incentives to reform SOEs under their control, due to a hardening of budget constraints and rising competition from non-state-owned enterprises. The privatization and restructuring of SOEs, based on 'seizing the large and releasing the small", led to opposite reforms at three highest and lowest levels of jurisdiction: at the township level full privatization of small SOEs and, at the central level, mergers, agglomerations, corporatization and listing of some large SOEs. In the middle there was no single template, with privatization of medium-sized SOEs at the county level, and mass SOE worker redundancies at the city level.

The privatization process in China has had three specific features. The first one, which differentiates it from what happened in the former Soviet economy and its satellites (Cao et al. 1999), is the limited role of liquidity and wealth constraints on buyers of privatized firms, due to the high-savings rate in China and the low net worth of its SME SOEs. Second, a substantial share of privatized firms incorporated in the form of employee/manager ownership were labelled 'stock cooperatives'. Third, privatization was associated with new investments which yielded both growth and profits. An implication of such features is that, in the Chinese case, resistance to privatization was minimized before the event, and, after it, stakeholders benefited from the process, ensuring its durability.

3.3.2   Motivations for Stock Market Creation

In the early 1990s the government found it urgent to stop relying exclusively on subsidies and bank loans for the financing of SOEs, and decided to build up the stock market. Banks were not able to provide long term funding for fixed capital investment by firms, like ten-year loans, since the

---

[5] Montinola et al. (1995), as the whole literature on that subject in China, use the term decentralization, but they actually mean deconcentration, which refers to the dispersion of control within one single hierarchical organization, and not to the transfer of control from one organization to another. Indeed in China, the local leaders are not chosen at the local level but appointed by the higher level of jurisdiction.

maturity of bank loans was exclusively short term (typically one year). From this point of view, while NPLs are a bad thing, they are good in as much as when the loan is not paid back the maturity mismatch of firms is suppressed. It is also difficult for banks to provide large loans which require approval from regional or national headquarters, while, with fast growth, such loans are needed for large-scale investment.

The too-high dependence on indirect or intermediated finance created many problems, such as low efficiency, corruption, rent seeking, and political and social externalities. Such dependence gave the authorities a huge incentive to move to direct financing, especially with NPLs and a soft budget constraint.

It would appear that the sources of financing considerably changed over time, from taxes to bank deposits and then to shares, thus involving two sequential moves: from subsidies to intermediated financed and then to direct finance. However, this change may be more apparent than real. Indeed, deposit financing as well as share financing, all appear as forms of implicit taxes (Gordon and Li 2003; Lai and Yang 2009), although when buying shares individuals are able to decide upon the financing decision, as previously they had no say in it. The change in the provision of funds involved a move from tax receipts pre-1984, to household savings (via bank deposits) with a very widespread coverage, and then to stock market investors' savings. Such investors were mostly individuals but represented only a subset of them, generally living in large, especially coastal, cities.

A major underlying precondition for direct finance is a rise in individual incomes and a high-saving rate, as well as a very low opportunity cost (interest rate on deposits), due to strict regulations in the context of financial repression. Individuals had a huge incentive to move their savings out of bank deposits, with low real return, to the stock market, with expected high returns (see Chap. 4), which explains the initial dominance of such individual investors in that market, given the lack of alternative investment opportunities like bonds or funds.

During his famous 'Southern Tour' in early 1992, Deng Xiaoping wondered to what extent stock markets were good or dangerous for China, and whether 'socialist China' could make use of them. He considered that they should be tried out on an experimental and temporary basis, enabling subsequent corrections or even gradual or immediate closure. This initial statement proved able to exert durably a strong influence on top leaders and regulators. Indeed, though expressed more than two-and-a-half decades ago, Deng's view still represents well the way in which the stock market is viewed by the current top leadership in China. From the very start, the creation of a stock market was indeed conceived in the PRC as an experiment which could be interrupted at any point of time. It is instructive to mention that, in the case of the government bond market, the upheavals of the first half of the 1990s led to the closure of both the bond futures and of the access of individual investors to the bond spot market. Accordingly, the short-termism in the behaviour of individual investors in the stock market was a built-in response to the uncertainty about the permanence of the market. At no point did the top leadership conceive of the stock market as an independent entity which would evolve according to standard principles.

However, in the new understanding of leaders in the second decade of the new millennium, the stock market seems to have become part and parcel of the Chinese financial system. Typically, in September 2015, three months after a large crash of the Chinese stock market, President Xi declared that the most important direction for Chinese economic reform is that the market shall play a determinant function and the government shall also play a better role. In his view, both the invisible and the visible hands have to be used. Even if the stock market goes up and down, it is its own regularity, and the government should not intervene. He emphasized that the responsibility of the government is to keep the openness, the fairness and market order, to protect investors, especially small- and medium-sized ones, and to promote stock market development steadily and in a sustainable way, to prevent a great panic. This implies that developing capital markets is the official objective of Chinese reform, and it will remain so, in spite of stock market volatility.

The listing of large SOEs from the mid-1990s bears some similarities with the 'government-supervised-and-merchant-managed' scheme, favoured by the late Qing government to try and kick-start industrial modernization, as detailed in Chap. 2. This scheme was already an attempt to side-step the funding constraints faced by a government, with limited tax revenues, to finance firms. The managers of firms held official ranks, the firms had to pay some official dividend even if standard dividends were not awarded, and local Qing government officials were strongly involved in supervising the companies while shareholders' meetings had no decision-making power.

3.3.3   Reform of State-Owned Banks

Reforming the financial system could not be limited to the creation and development of the stock market, given the dominant reliance on bank loans to finance the economy. The reform of the state banking system (Naughton 2007) took place in three steps which have become a guiding principle. These steps included: reducing non-performing loans, implementing the shareholding system, and then listing in stock markets.

Before 1997, the bank industry in China developed rapidly and accumulated tremendous risks, since the restructuring of large SOEs, still dominant in the economy, had not made substantial progress, and these firms had become more and more loss making. Many loans of the four state-owned banks became NPLs.

In 1994 the government decided to set up three Policy banks: the National Development Bank, the Import-Export Bank, and the Agriculture Development Bank. It tried to separate commercial financing (i.e. new loans, not outstanding ones) from policy-oriented financing, which was part of industrial policy in a form of directed credit. Even though, on paper, this looked like a good idea, in practice it did not differ much from the previous arrangements for two reasons. First, the only way the Policy banks could get funding was by issuing bonds bought by commercial banks. Second, *de facto* Commercial banks still had to grant loans to SOEs as part of the directed credit policy of the government. Anyway this reform did not at all address the second factor behind the low profitability of SOBs, that is, their multitask character, in as much as like all SOEs the SOBs had to fund their internal social safety net.[6]

Three major developments took place in the banking sector which newly brought competition to the SOBs and also started to provide new sources of financing for the private sector, a sector which was all but neglected by SOBs. First, from 1998 to 2002, the newly set up shareholding commercial banks, for example, Minsheng Bank, rapidly improved both their profitability and quality of assets, and made swift progress in corporate governance, financial products, and technological innovation, as well as in risk management. Obviously such banks were not multitask and did not have to buy bonds issued by Policy banks, so their profitability was high and they could easily out-compete SOBs in lending to the private sector. Second, the former Urban Credit Cooperatives (Girardin 1997), which were non-bank financial institutions like credit unions in the US,

---

[6]Among the few empirical works which have taken such social factors into account, Matthews et al. (2009) is noteworthy. They document that when allocative inefficiency is viewed as the optimal by-product of an allocation of resource inputs subject to employment constraints Chinese banks are similar to their western peers.

were restructured and merged into city commercial banks. Third, between 1996 and 2005 foreign banks were allowed to open branches in Beijing but only for foreign-currency business.

A two-pronged strategy was used by the government to deal with the flow and the stock issues faced by SOBs. First, in order to allow SOBs to both fulfill their multitasks and to handle the accumulation of NPLs, the government, in the late 1990s and for more than a decade and a half, fixed the loan-deposit interest rate spread between 5% and 7%, thus allowing SOBs to capture the profits of SOEs. Second, to address the problem of NPLs of the four major commercial banks, the central government established four asset management companies (AMCs) under the State Council in 1999, thus laying the foundation for the development of commercial banks into very large global banks.

In February 2002, the central government proposed that the SOBs should be modern financial enterprises and reorganized into state-controlled listed commercial banks. In 2003, the State Council decided to establish the China Banking Regulatory Commission (CBRC), to promulgate the Banking Supervision and Administration Law, to speed up the disposal of non-performing assets of SOBs, augment their capital, and create conditions for their listing.

In December 2003, the Central Huijin Investment Company was incorporated with the Ministry of Finance (MOF), and in January 2004 the central government injected 45 billion US$ (372.465 billion RMB) of foreign exchange reserves into its capital. In turn Huijin used this to inject capital into the Bank of China (BoC) and the China Construction Bank (CCB), and introduced foreign strategic partners. The BoC and the CCB corporations were formally established in August and September 2004 respectively. The Bank of Communications (BOC) was restructured from a shareholding commercial bank into a state-owned shareholding commercial bank, through financial restructuring, also in 2004. In April 2005 (November 2008) Huijin was allowed by the central government to invest US$15 billion (US$19 billion) in the Industrial and Commercial Bank of China, ICBC (Agricultural Bank of China, ABC).

After their establishment as shareholding companies, under the coordination of the financial supervision authority (FSA), the SOBs were very creative in the introduction of strategic investors. Strategic cooperation agreements were signed, in sequence, between BoC and HSBC in August 2004; CCB and Bank of America as well as Asia Financial Holdings, a wholly-owned subsidiary of Singapore's Temasek, in June-July 2005; BoC with Royal Bank of Scotland, Temasek, UBS Group and the Asian Development Bank, in August–October 2005; and ICBC with Goldman Sachs in January 2006. After the incorporation of ABC in 2009, due to the tensions in domestic and international capital markets at the time, no foreign strategic investor was involved, but only a few domestic financial investors.

On the basis of the successful restructuring and introduction of strategic investors, the four commercial SOBs launched very successful initial public offerings (IPOs) and stock listings: H-shares were listed in Hong Kong in June 2005 by BOC, in October 2005 by CCB, in June 2006 by BoC, in October 2006 by ICBC, and in July 2010 by ABC. In addition two SOBs made domestic IPOs in Shanghai, ICBC in October 2006, and ABC in July 2010. So far, the shareholding reform of the commercial SOBs has been successfully completed.

The reform of commercial SOBs, which lasted for more than a decade, not only solved the problem of huge NPLs, through the setting up of the AMCs, but also transformed the commercial SOBs, through incorporation, recapitalization, and listing. The government only slowly and belatedly reformed the fixed-interest-rate system after the listing of the big commercial banks, a system which siphoned off a big part of the profits of firms and became a big burden on the economy during the slowdown after 2010. In addition, the SOBs participated in the attraction of the best graduates in line with the rest of the Chinese financial industry. These two series of factors themselves fed back into a worsening of the economy, due to the drain on financial resources and human capital.

3.4   STOCK MARKET DEVELOPMENT

3.4.1   Institutional Evolution and Regulation

An effectively functioning stock market needs four major components: the exchange, the infrastructure, intermediaries and service firms, as well as regulatory authorities. In the case of the Chinese stock market it did not prove possible to set up all four components at once. The exchange was initially created, with no national regulation, some intermediaries, but hardly any infrastructure. Setting up laws and regulations at the very start would not have proved useful since it was first necessary to establish proper enforcement mechanisms and a culture of law-abiding behaviour.

A modern securities market is a multi-level system. The first is the core level, which mainly includes three elements: the demand side (investors), the supply side (listed companies) and the market itself (exchanges). The earliest stock exchanges came into being in the Netherlands in 1611, and Britain and France subsequently established their own stock exchanges. The New York Stock Exchange was established and operated by dealers and auctioneers under the 1792 Buttonwood Agreement (Geisst 1997). After two or three hundred years of development, the economic crisis and stock market crash of 1929–1933 in the United States made people realize the importance of supervision, law, and intermediary services, which generated the multi-layer complex structure of the modern securities market.

The different levels of China's securities market were gradually established by the government. In the early 1990s, the central government created the State Council Securities Commission (SCSC) and the China's Securities and Regulatory Commission (CSRC) to lead the whole process. The Ministry of Finance (MOF) was put in charge of formulating accounting standards and managing and standardizing relevant accounting firms. The Ministry of Justice (MOJ) became responsible for standardizing and managing relevant law firms. All laws and regulations concerning the securities market had to be considered and adopted by the National People's Congress. This constitutes a unique supervisory layer of China's securities market. Securities companies, accounting firms and law form and intermediate level. In the development of China's securities market, the CSRC attaches great importance to the construction of the infrastructure level, which mainly includes the establishment and regulation of new exchanges, the improvement of laws and regulations, and the establishment of self-regulatory organizations of securities, such as the China Securities Association and the China Futures Association (Fig. 3.1).

In China, like in most emerging markets, the government, and not the private sector, not only created the stock market but also carried on heavily influencing its operations. The dominant role of the CSRC was apparent in the creation of new exchanges and of institutional investors. The exchanges are de facto a subsidiary of the regulator, since their top leadership is appointed by the CSRC, and all the exchange regulations have to be approved by CSRC. Only implementation is left to the administration of the exchanges.

The government wants to keep control of the market via both regulations and state-owned institutional investors, such as insurance companies,

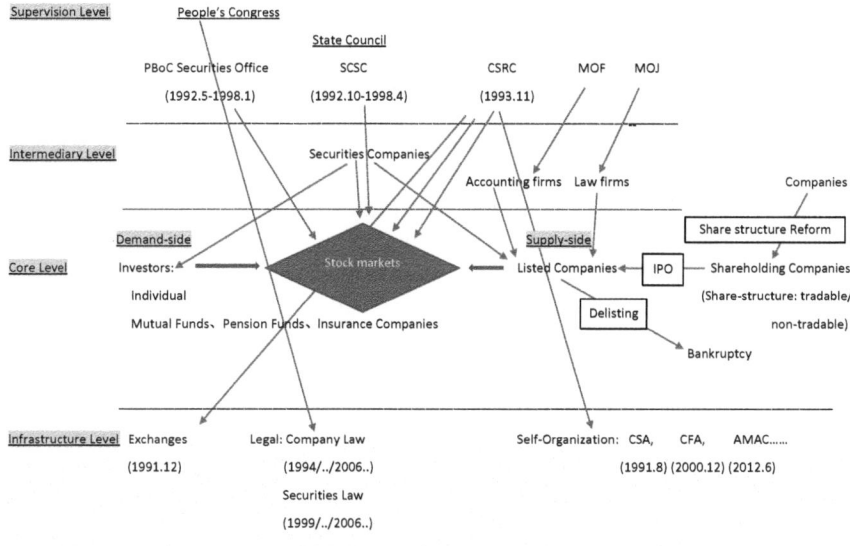

Fig. 3.1 Major components of China's stock market. Acronyms in the chart are defined as follows: AMAC (Assets Management Association), CFA (China Futures Association), CSA (China Securities Association), CSRC (China's Securities and Regulatory Commission), IPO (Initial Public Offering), MOF (Ministry of Finance), MOJ (Ministry of Justice), PBoC, and SCSC (China's State Council Securities Commission)

pension funds, social security funds, and the stock market stabilization fund (as well as possibly the sovereign wealth fund).

The CSRC has multiple objectives and finds it difficult to reach them all. According to the provisions of the Securities Law, the regulatory objectives of the CSRC are: regulating the issuance and trading of securities (maintaining market order); protecting the legitimate rights and interests of investors; maintaining social economic order and social public interests; and promoting the development of the market economy. There is not much difference here with international standards. However, in the practice of supervision, the CSRC has been excessively involved in coordinating macroeconomic regulation and control, supporting the development of the real economy, financing state-owned enterprises, and maintaining the stable development of the national economy. It has not spent as much effort in improving the relevant systems and measures to protect the legitimate interests of investors. In addition, law enforcement by the CSRC has been somewhat arbitrary, generating great doubts about the scope of its investigation of malpractices, and the intensity of punishment. In recent years, regulatory accountability has attracted the attention of policy makers.

The CSRC lacks the necessary instruments to intervene during a crisis. In 2015, the stock market experienced abnormal fluctuations. The government initially talked-up and stimulated a sharp rise in the market and the subsequent crash was partly triggered when state investors pulled out (see Chap. 4). Subsequently, under the coordination of the State Council, China's securities finance companies used funds (possibly amounting to more than 200 billion RMB) provided by the People's Bank of China (PBoC) to buy stocks, thus avoiding further falls in the stock market. The bubbke and crash in 2015 exposed the imperfect coordination mechanism between China's financial regulators.

The National Financial Conference, held in July 2017, proposed the establishment of the State Council Financial Stability Development Committee (the "Financial Stability Committee"), which was formally established in November 2017. One of its functions is to hold financial supervision departments to account. However, the specific working mechanism for the performance and accountability of financial regulatory agencies needs to be further developed and improved.

3.4.2   Investors

The Chinese stock market has been widely portrayed as featuring a very large number of retail investors. On the face of it the number of Individual investors indeed appears to have grown in an impressive way, when measured from the number of accounts, which from less than one million in the early 1990s, went over 60 million in the early new millennium (Walter and Howie 2006), to reach 200 million at the peak of the bubble, mid-2015. Not less than 30 million accounts were opened in the first semester of that year, two-thirds of which by holders who did not even hold a high-school degree. The number of accounts fell substantially after 2015, but remains high. Retail investors account for 85% of trades.

Such a large number of retail investors' accounts seems to have involved a very high proportion of double counting, since most investors would, at least initially, open an account both in Shenzhen and in Shanghai. Accounting for this may reduce by half the number of investors. Even that lower number should be discounted by the number of companies in which each shareholder holds shares. The true number of active accounts may be further reduced by between one-third and four-fifths. However, participants in initial public offerings (IPOs) correspond to an even lower number. Even the listings of the most popular giant companies, such as Baosteel and Sinopec, did not attract more than half a million investors (Walter and Howie 2006; Walter 2014).

Before 1998, in the absence of institutional investors,[7] the market was even more speculative. In the first half of the 1990s large players (*Zhuang Jia*) were cornering the market, contributing to high volatility. The term *Zuozhuang* means to corner the market. Subsequently such players responded to curbs put to their activities by CSRC by trying to distribute accounts geographically. The CSRC monitored both large trading orders and the holdings of branches of security companies when they were too concentrated. Large investors responded by using fake identity accounts, which CSRC again had to handle by checking investors' accounts. Accordingly, in 2005–2006 the number of accounts fell. Later on, in 2014–2015, individual investors had to report in person to the security company to be identified.

From the mid-1990s up to 1998 the very few investment funds were only close-ended. Subsequently open-ended funds were allowed. Over the 2001–2006 period, the big problem faced by the newly created mutual funds can be conveyed by the expression "mice which eat the storage" (*Laoshu cang*). Mutual fund managers first bought shares themselves and bid up the price with the mutual funds' money, and then sold the shares they held. CSRC set up a department of mutual fund supervision in 2003. In the mutual fund development process the CSRC has been playing a crucial role, in their creation and registration, the nature of products, the supervision of their daily operation, as well as regulations. Up to the end of 2018 there were 131 independent mutual funds, whose total assets under management were 13 trillion RMB. Among such funds are the Money Market Funds, the so-called 'bond-type' funds, which only invest in corporate and government bonds, and the stock funds.

Hedge funds were created in 2003 in China, in a disguised way, borrowing trading accounts from trust companies and mutual funds as special customers. This meant that hedge funds were constrained for ten years in their expansion, during which their number hardly grew. Subsequently,

---

[7] An overview of institutional investors is provided by Sun et al. (2015).

from 2013 onwards, hedge funds were legalized and their number started to expand in an explosive way in the subsequent two years.

In China, hedge funds can buy corporate bonds but mainly invest in equities. Over the last five years, the growth and decay of the number and activity of hedge funds has been closely associated with the ups and downs of the stock market. From around 100 in 2013, their active number grew to around several hundred in 2014, an amazing 17,000 in 2015, at the time of the market bubble (see Chap. 4), down to 10,000 in 2016, subsequent to the crash. The CSRC asked them to register, and half of them were closed in 2017.

Under the legal classification used in China up to mid-2018, hedge funds were grouped with private equity under the heading of private funds. There are currently 233 private funds which manage over 10 billion RMB—266 manage between 5 and 10 billion, 642 between 2 and 5 billion, 835 between 1 and 2 billion, and the rest manage either less than 1 billion or do not manage anything.

3.4.3   Intermediaries and Infrastructure

In the 1990s, securities firms enjoyed fast growth with no sound business model, no proper corporate governance, and no internal control measures, and speculated in the market. Many of them were involved in illegal activities, such as misappropriation of clients' capital and insider trading.

From 2002 to the end of 2003, CSRC imposed sanctions on eight securities firms. In August 2004, it took an extensive action plan to create a comprehensive governance framework for China's securities companies. CSRC used three key strategies: liquidation and restructuring of failed companies, stricter supervision or industry capacity building, and initiation of a comprehensive restructuring of securities firms. In July 2005, the State Council issued the Scheme for the Comprehensive Restructuring of Securities Firms, formulated by the CSRC, requiring the active cooperation and collaboration of local governments and relevant authorities. By the end of 2006, 31 securities firms were closed, including Southern Securities, Minfa Securities, Deheng Securities, and Guangdong Securities.

By the end of 2017 there were 131 shareholding security companies, including 11 joint ventures, 30 listed in Shanghai or Shenzhen, and 14 in Hong Kong. Their total assets were 614 trillion RMB and their net capital 1.58 trillion. The whole industry's profit in 2017 was 113 billion RMB, and their percentage commissions represented 0.0378%. Brokerage was their dominant source of revenue, with 82 billion, while their other source of revenue (such as asset management) represented only 31 billion. In the new millennium they were no more allowed to do proprietary trading, and their underwriting business became negligible, especially after the mid-2015 crash. The top five securities companies hold not far from one-third of the market for brokerage and asset management, as well as account for a similar share of assets, net profit or revenue. All securities companies lack any form of specialization and compete in all lines of business.

The government plays a critical role in the day-to-day functioning of markets, with the CSRC either deciding on regulations or approving those designed by the exchange.

The adoption of modern technology and a computerized automated order-matching trading system are the key characteristics of China's stock exchanges. Even though there are two trading systems, the Securities Trading Automated Quotations System (STAQS) and the National Electronic Trading System (NETS), most stocks are traded on the latter, a centralized and computerized order-driven system.

The rules of trading include intra-day 10% caps, imposed from 1996 onwards.[8] Since 1995 the trade settlement has been extremely quick, taking place at T+1. The opening hours, five days a week, run from 9:30 to 15:00, with a lunch break from 11.30 to 13.00. There is a pre-trading session from 9:15 to 9:25 each trading day.

Two trading methods are used by the order-matching system: a periodic auction and a continuous auction. The morning opening prices are generated by the periodic auction during the pre-trading session. After the morning opening, the trading mechanism stays the same during the rest of the day. There is thus a continuous market until closing.

All orders are valid for one day only. The smallest trading unit is 100 shares. The SHSE and SZSE use a single tick size, which is 0.01 RMB. Floor trading among member brokers is strictly prohibited, and short selling was initially not allowed. Any legally recognized transaction has to be carried out through the automated order-matching system. There is no market maker to stabilize stock prices by trading on its own account.

---

[8] Empirical work on the effects on China's stock market of intra-day price limits and trading halts includes Wan et al. (2018) and Xu et al. (2014). Chung et al. (2013) and Lao et al. (2018) provide a microstructure study and measures of liquidity. An early review of market organization is provided by Xu (2000).

3.4.4   Multi-layered Market

The consistency of gradual market design can be illustrated by the study of the recent stages of reforms and new market creations, such as the Small and Medium Enterprises board in 2004, the (free but immature and very hectic) Second Board for high-tech companies (Growth enterprises, GEM, or ChiNext[9]) in 2009, the latter featuring a lower entry threshold and looser conditions for listing than the former. As a rule, the initiative for setting up new types of exchanges came from local (city) governments, such as Shenzhen and Shanghai, but the implementation was often delayed considerably, since the central government did not give them its seal of approval (see Chap. 2).

Before 1998 the Shenzhen stock exchange played a more active role than the Shanghai one. To avoid competition with Shanghai, the Shenzhen local government wanted its stock exchange to focus on the Small and Medium Enterprises board. A proposal to that effect was made by the Shenzhen government in 2001, and as a gesture of goodwill it stopped IPOs in the Shenzhen main board. At the same time, the Shenzhen government proposed the GEM to enable an exit of venture capital[10] via listing. But, due to the different priorities of local and central governments, the proposal was frozen by the central government for three to four years. The GEM, seen as too speculative by the central government, was created only in 2011. After 2011, Shanghai reacted and proposed an international board (for companies such as Unilever) but this was not approved. The Shenzhen main board was marginalized, since all large firms moved to Shanghai. This is why investors now care only about the Shanghai composite index.

Institutional innovations of exchanges also involved local government interest. While commodities futures markets have been active for decades in China, no stock index futures market existed. After 2005 Shanghai proposed a Financial Futures[11] exchange for stocks, which it obtained in April

---

[9] China's GEM is examined in detail by Liu and Wang (2015).

[10] The venture capital industry started in the 1990s with foreign listed funds (Wang and Li 2015), and rose significantly in the new millennium with both private and government backed initiatives (Zhang and Mayes 2018). Ahlstrom and Bruton (2003) and Ahlstrom et al. (2007) emphasize that both the challenges encountered by venture capitalists and the nature of the investment framework employed in China differ markedly from those of the west.

[11] The development and problems of China's stock index futures are surveyed by Zhou (2015).

2010. Later, options on commodities futures contracts were set up, in 2017, and index options, in 2016 (not liquid enough, with only individual investors).

From 1982 onwards, some companies began to raise interest-bearing funds, either internally or from the public. These became the early form of corporate bonds. By the end of 1986, such unregulated bonds reached more than US$2.9 billion in outstanding value. In 1987, the State Council stipulated that further bond issuances would be subject to approval by the PBoC, and the quota of the total amount of annual corporate bonds issues would be set by the PBoC, the State Planning Commission (SPC), and MOF. In 1992, the total issuance reached a record high of US$12.7 billion, much more than the quota. In this fever of issuing corporate bonds, many enterprises did not prepare themselves to pay back the bonds on maturity, and many defaulted. Starting in 1993, the issuance of corporate bonds went through a long period of decline.

The issuance of corporate bonds is now regulated by the National Development and Reform Commission (NDRC). The NDRC previously regulated SOE issuance of such bonds through a formal verification and approval process, but in 2015 it relaxed the guidelines, allowing the issuance of corporate bonds with a simple registration process. The State Council determines the approved size of the issuance. The issuer determines the interest rate after taking into account market conditions. While there are no restrictions on term, there are normally few long-term issuances with maturities longer than 5 years.

After only a few decades of expansion, the Chinese bond market[12] became the third largest in the world in 2016. Issuance to date has generally been dominated by government and public sector bonds issued by government affiliated companies, which account for about 69% of the bonds outstanding. However, at the margin, corporate bond issuance has been growing and has the potential to reach 40% of total outstanding volumes, over the next five years. At the end of 2005, corporate bonds

---

[12] The corporate bond market consists of the following types of instruments: Corporate bonds, typically those of SOEs, issued on the interbank bond market (21% of the market); Commercial papers (17%) and medium-term notes (29%) issued by domestic companies and regulated by the National Association of Financial Market Institutional Investors (NAFMII); and Corporate bonds (18%) issued by a whole range of private sector issuers and listed on either the SSE or SZSE, regulated by the CSRC. Issuance standards vary widely among different types of bonds. Corporate bond issuance process is still based on a quota, which is prone to great administrative influence.

accounted for just 7.2% of the total Chinese bond market. Their share grew to over 30% at of the end of 2016, in a market which has expanded ten-fold. The outstanding bond issues of government-affiliated policy banks, financial sector bonds (including those of the four commercial SOBs) and other banks/financial bonds, account for a little over one fifth of the Chinese bond market, second only to government bonds.

3.4.5   Split-share Reform

The split-share reform helped to solve the complicated shareholding structure problems in China's stock markets. Previously, unequal ownership rights were given to the shareholders of state-owned shares, legal person shares, and collective or individual shares. These shares were priced differently, sometimes on parallel markets. This differential treatment led to a very sizable proportion of non-tradable shares, with a float much lower than capitalization. The listed companies promised, in the IPO prospectus, or the public announcement for listing, that the shares owned by the (Legal person and State) shareholders prior to the public offering would remain unlisted and non-tradable. This really blocked the development of China's stock markets. With the increasing issuance of new shares, the need to align the float on capitalization became increasingly obvious from 2001 onwards. Before 2004, there were several attempts to reduce the number of state-owned shares through the sales of such shares on the market, which were later suspended for various reasons. At the end of 2004, 64% of the total listed Chinese companies' shares were non-tradable, and three fourths of those companies were state-owned. The postponement of that reform was one of the underlying reasons for the lasting bear market in the first half of the 2000s.

A major step towards a more complete market was the implementation of this much-delayed split-share reform between Spring 2005 and Spring 2008 (Beltrati et al. 2012). The reform was based on market-oriented principles with "centralized organization and decentralized decision-making". In practice, the holders of non-tradable shares generally compensated the holders of tradable shares by giving out a portion of their shares at mutually-agreed prices. No government intervention or price-setting was imposed. The process started with a proposal put forward by the holders of non-tradable shares, which would then be revised by all shareholders, followed by a vote on the proposal by all shareholders and by holders of tradable shares. The proposal could only be passed if at least two-thirds of the shareholders voted in favour of, and at least two-thirds of holders of tradable shares endorsed, the proposal, a measure aimed at protecting the interest of small investors in the negotiation process. The last step involved the formal approval of the terms of the agreement by CSRC. Listed companies planning to float non-tradable shares could take measures to stabilize share prices when necessary.

3.4.6   Opening Up

The external opening-up of China's capital markets became an important issue after China was admitted to the WTO in December 2001. In December 2002, the Qualified Foreign Institutional Investor (QFII) program allowed licensed foreign institutional investors to trade A-shares on the secondary market. By August 2018, 316 foreign institutional investors had been granted QFII status, and allocated a quota totalling US$100.257 billion. The QFII program has raised the international profile of China's securities market and started to change the landscape of competition in the fund management industry.

The Qualified Domestic Institutional Investor (QDII) program, launched in May 2006, allowed licensed domestic institutional investors to invest in overseas markets. By April 2018, 143 fund management firms and securities firms had been granted QDII status and an aggregate investment quota of US$98.3 billion. The introduction of the QDII program helped to some extent to balance supply and demand in the foreign exchange market and started to provide Chinese investors with opportunities to invest in international capital markets with a broader range of products.

The Rules for the Establishment of Securities Firms with Foreign Investment and the Rules for the Establishment of Sino-foreign Joint Venture Fund Management Companies were issued in 2002. By the end of 2017, China had 13 Sino-foreign securities firms and 44 Sino-foreign fund management companies, of which 19 firms had foreign ownership holdings above 40%. In addition, China Galaxy Futures and ABN-AMRO set up the first Sino-foreign futures joint venture in 2006, marking the start of foreign participation in China's futures market.

The "Stock Connect" link between China's mainland markets and international stock markets (Hegde and Peng 2017), such as the Hong Kong and London Stock Exchanges, relaxes restrictions that historically split the Chinese stock market between shares targeted at local investors and those available to international investors. The link was first launched in November 2014 between the Shanghai and Hong Kong exchanges and was extended to the Shenzhen Stock Exchange in late 2016. It allows mainland Chinese investors to purchase selected Hong Kong and Chinese companies listed in Hong Kong, and lets foreigners buy China A-shares listed in the mainland in a less restrictive manner than previously.

For instance, the Shanghai-Hong-Kong stock connect allows overseas investors to trade eligible A-shares listed in Shanghai and eligible domestic investors to trade eligible H-shares listed in Hong Kong. To be eligible, investors are required to hold securities and cash accounts amounting at least to half-a-million RMB. Eligible shares both ways include those of dual-listed firms in Shanghai and Hong Kong (close to 70 securities), the constituents of the large- and medium-cap indices in Hong Kong (close to 270 securities), as well as of the 180 and 380 indices in Shanghai (close to 570 securities). The daily quota is capped at slightly above 10 billion RMB in each direction.

The Stock Connect programmes create a single 'China' stock market that ranks as one of the biggest in the world by market capitalization and daily trading turnover. For international investors, the programmes add more than 1400 companies to the investable universe. These moves may help diversify the portfolios of Chinese investors, bring closer the different prices[13] of dual-listed Chinese companies (see Chap. 4), and increase the likelihood of Chinese shares being included in global benchmark stock indexes.

In comparison with the earlier QDII and QFII schemes, which are still active in parallel with the Connect scheme, the latter benefits from more freedom, larger quotas, as well as lower transaction costs. Major novelties of the Connect scheme include both the involvement of individual investors and the lack of eligibility criteria with respect to the size of institutional investors.

The internationalization of China's stock market received a boost with its inclusion in global indices. In June 2018, global equities index compiler MSCI announced the inclusion of China's A-shares in its benchmark

---

[13] Price convergence should be helped by the Connect program but is weakened by a strong regulatory regime and large demand shocks (Hegde and Peng 2017). The price gaps of cross-listed stocks still persist after the Connect but are increasing at a slower speed. Similar patterns are found in the turnover, volatility, and liquidity gaps of the two markets. See also Kashyap (2016).

Emerging-Markets index (with a 0.7% weight to rise to 3.3% by Autumn 2019), on top of the 31% weight of overseas-listed Chinese firms. In the same month, FTSE Russell announced its decision to add the Chinese mainland's RMB-denominated A-shares to its global equity benchmarks, in phases starting in June 2019. With the inclusion of A-shares in key global benchmark indices, China's stock market will become a significant market which global fund managers should not neglect. Added foreign capital is likely to account for nearly 10% of China's A-share market capitalization over the next 10 years.

3.5 SUMMARY AND CONCLUSIONS

Establishing and developing a stock market is a complex and lengthy process. The historical experience of western countries suggests that this process may take 100 to 200 years. This lengthy process is mainly due to the multiple aspects of the development of the stock market: the establishment and operation of the exchange, the regulation of market transactions and settlement, the education of investors, the improvement in the quality of listed companies, and the setting up of financial intermediaries, as well as of law and accounting firms. During the development of China's stock market in the past three decades, the government has played a dominant role in all these aspects. In spite of, and/or thanks to, this dominant role, the Chinese stock market has developed into the world's second largest. We expect that it will continue to grow and mature in the future, but the continuation or weakening of the, *de facto*, if not *de jure*, dominant role of the government is an open issue.

REFERENCES

Acemoglu, D. 2013. The Future of Chinese Growth: Institutional Perspectives. MIT, Manuscript, December.

Ahlstrom, D., and G.D. Bruton. 2003. An Institutional View of China's Venture Capital Industry: Explaining the Difference Between China and the West. *Journal of Business Venturing* 18: 233–259.

Ahlstrom, D., G.D. Bruton, and K.S. Yeh. 2007. Venture Capital in China: Past, Present and Future. *Asia Pacific Journal of Management* 24 (3): 247–268.

Allen, F., J. Qian, and M. Qian. 2005. Law, Finance, and Economic Growth in China. *Journal of Financial. Economics* 77: 57–116.

Bai, C.-E., D. Li, Z. Tao, and Y. Wang. 2000. A Multitask Theory of State Enterprise Reform. *Journal of Comparative Economics* 28: 716–738.

Bai, C.-E., J. Lu, and Z. Tao. 2006. The Multitask Theory of State Enterprise Reform: Empirical Evidence from China. *American Economic Review* 96 (2): 353–357.

———. 2009. How Does Privatization Work in China? *Journal of Comparative Economics* 37: 453–470.

Bai, C.-E., and L.C. Xu. 2005. Incentives for CEOs with Multitasks: Evidence from Chinese State-owned Enterprises. *Journal of Comparative Economics* 33: 517–539.

Beltrati, A., B. Bortolotti, and M. Caccavaio. 2012. The Stock Market Reaction to the 2005 Split Share Structure Reform in China. *Pacific Basin Finance Journal* 20: 543–560.

Bowles, P., and G. White. 1993. *The Political Economy of China's Financial Reforms: Finance in Late Development*. Boulder, CO: Westview Press.

Cao, Y., Y. Qian, and B.R. Weingast. 1999. From Federalism, Chinese Style, to Privatization, Chinese Style. *Economics of Transition* 7 (1): 103–131.

Chung, H., C. Gao, J. Lu, and B. Misrach. 2013. An Empirical Analysis of the Shanghai and Shenzhen Limit Order Book. *Economic Modelling* 34: 37–41.

Du, J., and C. Xu. 2005. Market Socialism or Capitalism? Evidence from Chinese Financial Market Development. IEA Roundtable on Market and Socialism, April.

Fewsmith, J. 1994. *Dilemmas of Reform in China: Political Conflict and Economic Debate*. London: M.E. Sharpe.

Geisst, C.R. 1997. *Wall Street: A History*. Oxford: Oxford University Press.

Gerschenkron, A. 1962. *Economic Backwardness in Historical Perspective*. Cambridge: Harvard University Press.

Girardin, E. 1997. *Banking Sector Reform and Credit Control in China*. Paris: Development Centre Studies, OECD Development Centre.

Gordon, Roger H., and Wei Li. 2003. Government as a Discriminating Monopolist in the Financial Market: The Case of China. *Journal of Public Economics* 87 (2): 283–312.

Harwood, A., and B.L.R. Smith, eds. 1997. *Sequencing?* Washington, DC: Brookings Institution Press.

Hegde, S., and J. Peng. 2017. One Security, Two Prices: Evidence on Stock Market Bubbles from the Shanghai-Hong Kong Connect Program. Department of Finance, University of Connecticut, Manuscript, June.

Hoskin, K., and R. Macve. 2012. Contesting the Indigenous Development of "Chinese Double-entry Bookkeeping" and Its Significance in China's Economic Institutions and Business Organization Before c.1850. Working Paper No. 156/12, London School of Economics, Department of Economic History.

Hsieh, C.-T., and Z. Song. 2015. Grasp the Large, Let Go of the Small: The Transformation of the State Sector in China. *Brookings Papers on Economic Activity* 1: 295–346.

Jarai, Z. 1989. The Goals and Conditions for Setting up a Stock Market in Hungary. *European Economic Review* 33 (2–3): 448–455.

Kashyap, R. 2016. Hong Kong-Shanghai Connect/Hong Kong Beijing Disconnect (?): Scaling the Great Wall of Chinese Securities Trading Costs. *The Journal of Trading* 11 (3): 81–134.

Kornai, J. 1980. *Economics of Shortage*, 2 vols. Amsterdam: North Holland.

Lai, S.W., and Y. Yang. 2009. From Scorned to Loved? The Political Economy of the Development of the Stock Market in China. *Global Economic Review* 38 (4): 409–429.

Lange, O., and F. Taylor. 1938. *On the Economic Theory of Socialism*. Minneapolis: University of Minnesota Press.

Lao, L., S. Tian, and Q. Zhao. 2018. Will Order Imbalances Predict Stock Returns in Extreme Market Situations? Evidence from China. *Emerging Markets Finance and Trade* 54: 921–934.

Lin, Z.L. 1992. Chinese Double-entry Bookkeeping Before the Nineteenth Century. *Accounting Historians Journal* 19 (2): 103–122.

Liu, M., and J. Wang. 2015. Development, Problems and Suggestions for China's GEM. In *The Chinese Stock Market*, ed. S. Cheng and Z. Li, vol. 1, 368–410. Basingstoke: Palgrave Macmillan.

Matthews, K., Z. Xiao, and X. Zhang. 2009. Rational Cost Inefficiency in Chinese Banks. Working Paper 29/2009, Hong Kong Institute for Monetary Research.

McKinnon, R.I. 1993. *The Order of Liberalization/Financial Control in the Transition to a Market Economy*. 2nd ed. Johns Hopkins University Press.

Montinola, G., Y. Qian, and B. Weingast. 1995. Federalism, Chinese Style: The Political Basis for Economic Success in China. *World Politics* 48 (1): 50–81.

Naughton, B. 2007. *The Chinese Economy: Transition and Growth*. Cambridge, MA: MIT Press.

Nuti, D.M. 1989. Remonetization and Capital Markets in the Reform of Centrally Planned Economies. *European Economic Review* 33 (2–3): 427–458.

Perkins, D.H. 2019. Measuring China's Economic Reform Progress. *China Economic Review* 53 (1): 342–350.

Pistor, K., and C. Xu. 2005. Governing Stock Markets in Transition Economies: Lessons from China. *American Law and Economics Review* 7 (1): 184–210.

Roland, G. 2000. *Transition and Economics: Politics, Markets and Firms*. Cambridge, MA: MIT Press.

Sun, Y., Z. Zheng, and H. Dong. 2015. Institutional Investors in Chinese Stock Markets. In *The Chinese Stock Market Volume 1: A Retrospect and Analysis from 2002*, ed. S. Cheng and Z. Li, 106–186. Palgrave Macmillan.

Walter, C. 2014. Was Deng Xiaoping Right? An Overview of China's Equity Markets. *Journal of Applied Corporate Finance* 26 (3): 8–19.

Walter, C., and F. Howie. 2006. *Privatizing China: Inside China's Stock Markets*. New York: Wiley.

Wan, Y.-L., G.-J. Wang, Z.-Q. Jiang, W.-J. Xie, and W.-X. Zhou. 2018. The Cooling Off Effect of Price Limits and Trading Halts. *Physica A* 505: 153–163.

Wang, L., and B. Li. 2015. Venture Capital: Research Status and Prospects for the Future. *Journal of Economics and Public Finance* 1 (1): 60–91.

Wu, J. 2005. *Understanding and Interpreting Chinese Economic Reform*. Mason: Thompson.

Xu, C.K. 2000. The Microstructure of the Chinese Stock Market. *China Economic Review* 11: 79–97.

Xu, H.-C., W. Zhang, and Y.-F. Liu. 2014. Short-term Reaction After Trading Halts in the Chinese Stock Market. *Physica A* 401: 101–111.

Zhang, Y., and D.G. Mayes. 2018. The Performance of Governmental Venture Capital Firms: A Life Cycle Perspective and Evidence from China. *Pacific Basin Finance Journal* 48: 162–185.

Zhou, Z. 2015. Development and Problems of Stock Index Futures and Margin Trading and Short Selling in China. In *The Chinese Stock Market*, ed. S. Cheng and Z. Li, vol. 1, 313–367. Basingstoke: Palgrave Macmillan.

CHAPTER 4

A Chinese Style Speculative Market

Abstract Analyses of the functioning of China's stock market typically emphasize three major anomalies, all associated with departures from the informationally efficient market hypothesis.

The inherently speculative nature of the market, with recurrent bubbles, is the major anomaly, usually linked to major characteristics of that market involving the dominance of unsophisticated investors, binding short-sale constraints, and often costly arbitrage.

Exotic seasonalities represent the second recurrent anomaly. A Red-May effect, featuring the highest monthly returns every year in the spring, stands in sharp contrast to the January effect which rules in most major stock markets, and seems linked to the seasonal behaviour of credit awarded by banks.

Third, the segmentation, leading to a higher price of the domestic listed versus the foreign listed shares of Chinese mainland companies, represents the so-called puzzle of the Chinese stock market. It is an opposite premium to that characterizing multiple listings of other countries' companies. This puzzle is still present after repeated timid attempts at moving away from a rigid currency peg or at the gradual lifting of capital controls.

Keywords Speculation • Puzzles • Seasonality • Share-price premia • Opening-up

© The Author(s) 2019
E. Girardin, Z. Liu, *Demystifying China's Stock Market*,
https://doi.org/10.1007/978-3-030-17123-0_4

63

4.1   Introduction

In a country where financial development is still ongoing it is hardly possible for the stock market to behave according to the theory of informationally-efficient markets (Fama 1970), with prices fully reflecting all publicly available information and being unpredictable on the basis of existing regularities. The Chinese stock market is no exception to this rule,[1] being characterized by many anomalies, such as recurrent bubbles, exotic seasonalities and a variety of share-price premia between different segments of the market. The stability over time of such anomalies is unlikely, in the context of changes in major features, such as regulation, the attitude of regulators, the behaviour of investors, as well as the importance of institutional investors.

Given the limited alternative investment opportunities, initially a reduced float, still binding short-sale constraints, underpriced initial public offerings (IPOs), and a domination of unsophisticated investors, China's stock market combines all the ingredients to make it highly speculative. This speculative character was in some way built into the market from the start.

A well-known, and resilient, source of inefficiency in major stock markets around the world has been the so-called January effect, whereby stock returns are higher in January than in any other month of the year. China's stock market singles itself out by departing from such a regularity. The highest monthly returns are rather to be found in the spring, and thus labelled the 'Red-May' effect.

Segmentation has been a major feature of China's stock markets. This market has been divided between two segments, among which the largest one, the A-market, denominated in RMB, was initially reserved to, often immature, domestic investors, while the B-market, denominated in foreign currency, was initially restricted to foreign investors. The gap in price and performance between these two segments has, for long, puzzled many observers.

Due to highly binding capital controls, the multiple listing of Chinese firms on both domestic and foreign stock exchanges has resulted in an alphabet soup of premia. The major one has involved the Hong Kong stock market, where the stocks of mainland firms, so-called H-shares, represent a dominant part of the Hang-Seng index. Trying to explain the

---

[1] See Groenewold et al. (2004) and Malkiel (2007).

premium between the prices of A-shares and H-shares has occupied an abundant literature.

4.2   SPECULATION

4.2.1   What Attracts Investors to the Market?

On the face of it there is little incentive for investors to invest in the Chinese stock market, since a long-run buy-and-hold strategy, as recommended by Siegel (2014) for advanced countries' markets, would have generated zero real cumulative returns over two and a half decades, as documented by Allen et al. (2014). Figure 4.1 updates and confirms this finding.

Observers would like to know the nature of the incentives of domestic individual-household investors to trade shares in the Chinese stock market, and even more so, of foreign investors. With zero real cumulated long-run performance, dividend distribution neither regular nor sizeable, and the inability to sell for a long time due to the presence of non- tradable shares, what is it that keeps the clients coming? Investors would have

Fig. 4.1   Real Shanghai stock market index (in logarithm): 1990(12)–2018(12). Shanghai composite index (Source: Bloomberg) deflated by Consumer price index (Source: National Bureau of Statistics), base 1990(12) = 100. Monthly data

to be risk-lovers, or their behavior would need to be explained by gambling pleasure. But even gamblers get their pleasure from possible big winnings, and such big gains only appear very infrequently. Besides, gambling in China, officially prohibited, even in its unofficial guise, does not seem to be more frequent than in many other regions in the world (Binde 2005).

Average returns, computed on the Shanghai A-shares index with moving windows of one day to ten years, especially corrected for risk (Sharpe ratio), provide the answers to this puzzle (Table 4.1). The best holding period is of a quarter or half-a-year duration based on the adjusted or unadjusted Sharpe ratio. The returns even corrected for opportunity cost and fee give a misleading longer optimum holding time, that is, a year. If investors are trapped, in order to reach a higher adjusted Sharpe ratio, it is better for them to wait for another four or five years before selling their shares. It is not advisable to hold stocks for a longer period than five years since the Sharpe ratio drops subsequently very substantially. Accordingly a decade(s)-long buy-and-hold strategy as recommended by Siegel (2014) for other markets is not advisable for China.

Table 4.1 Shanghai composite returns and Sharpe ratio at different horizons (%)

Investment horizon	Annualized return	Sharpe ratio annualized	Annualized excess return after fee	Sharpe ratio annualized on excess returns and net of fee
Day	18.4	47.2	−36.0	−92.0
Week	19.9	43.3	5.9	13.3
Month	18.9	39.9	12.5	26.4
Quarter	21.2	37.3	16.4	28.7
Semester	21.7	37.0	17.3	29.5
1 year	25.9	28.8	21.7	24.1
2 years	23.5	23.6	19.4	19.4
3 years	15.8	27.0	11.7	19.9
4 years	14.4	30.9	10.3	22.0
5 years	13.8	31.5	9.8	22.3
6 years	10.5	17.1	6.5	10.5
7 years	14.0	22.2	10.0	15.9
8 years	13.7	23.0	9.7	16.3
9 years	15.4	19.7	11.4	14.6
10 years	16.2	17.0	12.2	12.8

Commission 0.2%, and risk free rate 4% in columns 3 and 4. Rolling computation for one day and up to 10-year holding periods for Shanghai A-shares (Source: Wind): January 1991–February 2019

We can read from these results that the smartest investors would usually hold their stock for three to six months, while the less smart, which may be the most numerous, would hold them for longer, up to four or five years. Interestingly, such a buy-and-hold strategy gives listed SOEs a lot of time to improve their performance to help their share price recover before their next seasoned equity offering (SEO).

The interval between peak returns is regularly four to six years long (Fig. 4.2). Participants, who have experienced large capital-gain opportunities so distant in time, are tempted to jump on signs of bubbles. Individual investors are then rational to rush in but of course they do not know when to exit, given that the duration of bubbles is very uneven (Sect. 4.2.2).

The bank deposit rate has been higher than yearly stock returns only when the latter were negative (with the only exception of 1993), as shown in Fig. 4.2. Not all investors can access the bond market, since individual investors are not eligible to buy bonds. Still it is noteworthy that the return on the Shanghai stock market (composite index) has been higher

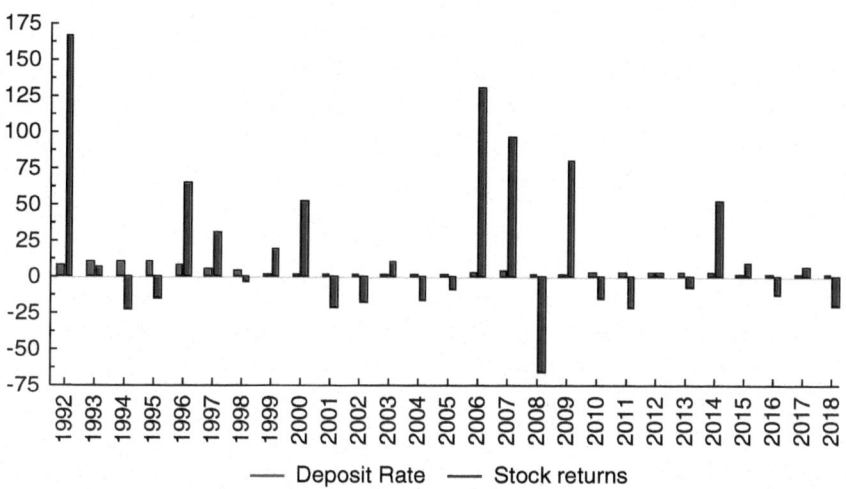

Fig. 4.2 Yearly return: stock market and bank deposits (%): 1992–2018. Yearly stock returns (Shanghai composite) exclusive of dividends (Source: Bloomberg) and one-year bank deposits (Source: International Financial Statistics, International Monetary Fund). Yearly data

than the government bond yield (at 5-year maturity) by 5% on average (2006–2017), giving rise to an equity premium.

4.2.2   Bubbles

Speculation is a major candidate to explain the breakdown of the link between stock prices and fundamentals. In the presence of both heterogeneous beliefs and short sale constraints, investors may have an incentive to pay too much for a stock if they expect to sell it in the future to another investor who will be willing to pay even more (Scheinkman and Xiong 2003; Hong et al. 2006). Accordingly, asset prices may contain a sizeable speculative component, which manifests itself by large trading volume and high return volatility; volume representing a proxy for irrational traders and speculative activity (see Scherbina and Schlusche 2014, for a general survey of the theory).

China's stock markets combine many of the ingredients of a highly speculative market. The first is an initial dominance of inexperienced individual investors (new to stock trading) who had very few other investment opportunities, especially before the creation of a residential housing market in the late 1990s. There is no direct access to the bond market for individuals whose main avenue for parking their savings is still time-deposits. Moreover, these individual investors are less informed, more subject to behavioural biases than institutional investors, and sentiment driven[2] (Bailey et al. 1999). The second ingredient is short-sales constraints, given the (initial) prohibition of short-selling.[3] The third ingredient is a small asset float, because prior to the split-share reform the state kept a substantial part of company shares, which were not tradable (Chap. 3), implying a sharp gap between float and capitalization. All these ingredients resulted in high share turnover despite high transaction costs.

The initial very high volatility, up to the mid-1990s, is striking in Fig. 4.3, which represents the daily range (logarithm of High/Low) for the Shanghai A-share index. Transaction volume was very low up until 2006. It rose in one step (Fig. 4.4) to a substantial level from 2007 to

---

[2] Sentiment is a positive source of momentum in China (Li and Yeh 2011; and Kang et al. 2002 for earlier evidence) but this may apply only in the short run with contrarian effects in the long run (Han and Li 2017). The role of sentiment is confirmed with social network data (Guo et al. 2017). Overreaction and asymmetric cognitive biases seem to be present in the A-share market (Ni et al. 2015).

[3] Short-selling only started to be allowed in the 2010s (see Sharif 2013; Zhou 2015).

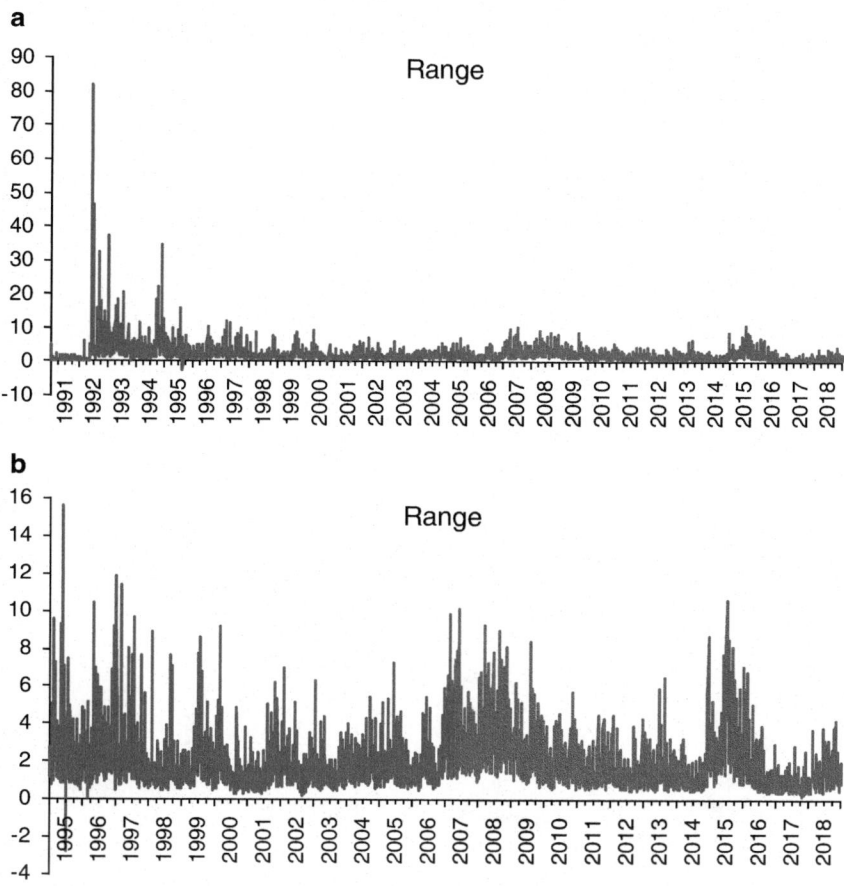

Fig. 4.3 Range volatility in the Shanghai A-share market. Daily data Shanghai A-share market (Source: Wind): Logarithm (High/Low) in %: (a) since the early 1990s (12/19/1990–12/28/2018); (b) since the mid-1990s (1/02/1995–12/28/2018)

mid-2014, skyrocketed during the bubble of 2014–2015, and then decreased and stabilized at a higher level than before the bubble.

A number of deep reforms may have lessened the speculative character of China's stock market. First, an expanding number of listed firms are more and more representative of an economy featuring increasingly dominant non-state-owned firms in industrial activity, restructured state-owned

a

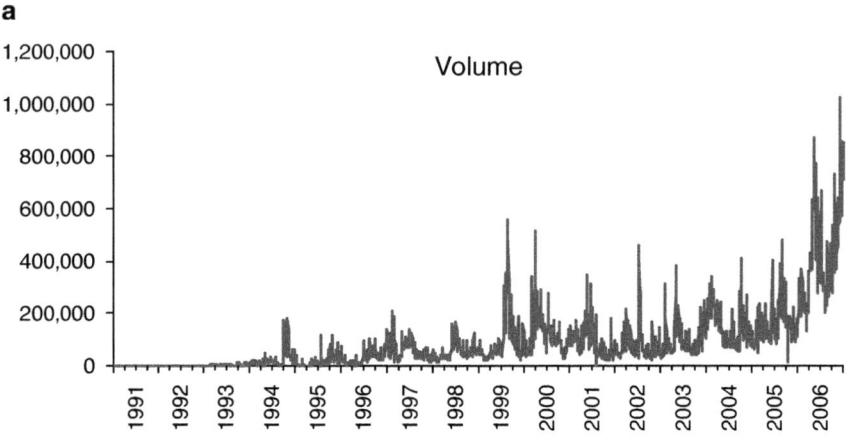

b

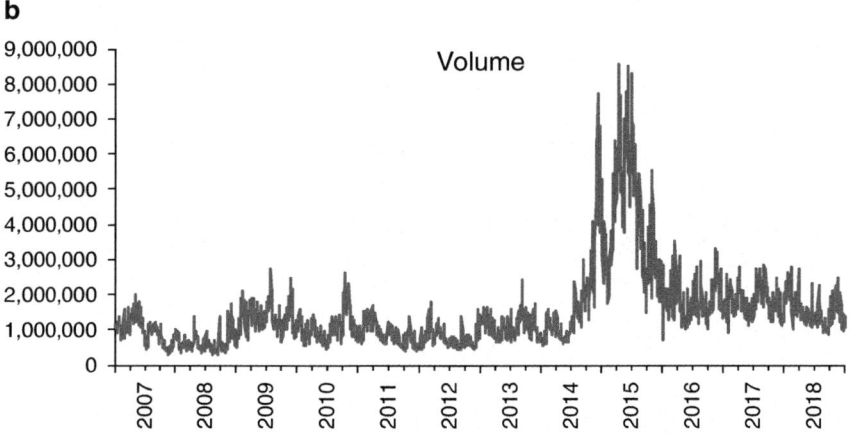

Fig. 4.4 Transaction volume in the Shanghai A-share index: 1990–2018. Daily data, Shanghai A-share market: (a) 12/19/1990–12/29/2006, (b) 1/04/2007–12/28/2018 (Source: Wind)

firms, as well as reforms associated with entry into the World Trade Organization (WTO) in December 2001. Second, the split-share reform initiated in May 2005 and completed late 2006, reduced the sharp hiatus between the float and the capitalization of the stock market by awarding compensating shares to non-state shareholders, as reviewed in Chap. 3. In the second decade of the new millennium the relaxation of the short-sales constraint, as well as the opening of a stock-index futures market, represented further steps in the reform process.

The asset price P_t can be modelled as comprising two components: a market fundamental (F_t) and a bubble (B_t) such that

$$P_t = F_t + B_t \qquad (4.1)$$

The bubble B_t is itself a sub-martingale process (Diba and Grossman 1988) such that:

$$E_t\left(B_{t+1}\right) = \frac{1}{\rho}B_t \quad \text{with} \quad \frac{1}{\rho} > 1. \qquad (4.2)$$

where ρ is the discount factor. The bubble process is specified as explosive with an autoregressive coefficient $(1/\rho)$, while the fundamental and the unobservable factors are themselves assumed to be at most integrated of order one.

Studies of China's stock market returns have distinguished bear and bull episodes (Chi et al. 2016), but only rarely speculative regimes. The latter were found, in the first decade of the market, to have arisen in the first half of 1995, for more than a year from the second quarter of 1996, as well as in late Spring 1999 and late Winter 2000 (Girardin and Liu 2003). The links between fundamentals and the stock market in China were examined both for prices and volatility. Bondt et al. (2010) considered the influence of conventional fundamentals in the spirit of Shiller's (1981) present value model. They showed that equity market reforms and excess liquidity drove episodes of stock price misalignments in the 2000s, especially from late 2006 to early 2008, and in mid-2009. A mixed-frequency approach, combining daily stock data and the monthly fundamental one, showed the presence of links between market-specific or macroeconomic fundamentals and long-run volatility in China's stock market (Girardin and Joyeux 2013).

It is important to search for a possible link between China's stock market and real economy. This task is made difficult by the sharp mismeasurement biases, from which macroeconomic activity data suffer in

China (Wu 2011). However, it is still worth considering, at a monthly frequency, the possible closeness in the cyclical movements of stock prices with the business cycle extracted from official industrial output data. Indeed, the market participants may be expected to focus on the official data, since alternative measures of activity have not been widely (or only recently) available. Over the first decade of the stock market (Fig. 4.5), the cyclical part of the stock index seems to have been able to lead the output cycle, especially at the time of the East Asian crisis, leading the 1999 output trough by around a year, and again in 2001 with a shorter lead time. From late 2004 onwards, the two series seem to have moved together, with the exceptions of the pre Global Financial crisis period (2005–2006), the period preceding (2013–2014) and during the 2015 bubble (see below), as well as in late 2017 and 2018. The simultaneous expansion (late 2006 to late 2007), collapse (2008) and recovery (2009) in the stock market and output are especially striking.

The empirical work on stock market bubbles went through two successive steps. The first one attempted to detect bubbles, while the second one

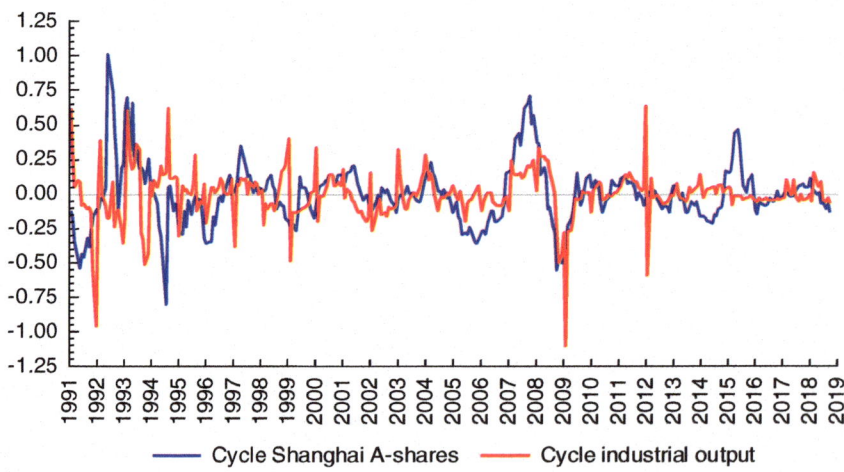

Fig. 4.5 Stock market and real economic activity: 1991(1)–2018(12). Cyclical component extracted with a Hodrick and Prescott (1997) filter (Lambda equals 14,400) for the Shanghai A-share index (Source: Wind) and the official industrial value added data (Source: The Conference Board). The cycle is multiplied by ten for the latter

tried to date their beginning and end. The detection of bubbles has mainly searched for duration-dependence, in which the presence of speculative bubbles is inferred from a long-lasting run of positive abnormal returns (McQueen and Thorley 1994)). Such a run is itself associated with negative duration dependence, that is, the longer the bubble has lasted the higher is its probability of bursting. For mainland China, such tests have produced mixed, and often contradictory, results (see the survey in Girardin et al. 2018). Indeed, evidence of duration dependence appears sensitive to: the choice of sample periods; the frequency of the data (weekly vs. monthly); the method of correcting for discrete observations of continuous duration; and the use of value-weighted versus equally-weighted portfolios (Harman and Zuehlke 2004).

A second line of research has proved increasingly appealing, due to its ability to provide a dating of the start and end of speculative episodes. This bubble-dating technique aims at detecting precisely when the price starts and stops exploding, that is, a given price in the current period is associated to an even higher price in the next period.[4] Such an explosive-root test, run on a moving window (Phillips et al. 2014, 2015), enables a real-time detection of bubbles.[5] It is desirable for a bubble test to use data of a frequency higher than one month, such as weekly, since bubbles usually do not last very long, and a bubble from the middle of one month to the middle of the following month would be missed with monthly data. Stock market bubble tests attempt to control for fundamentals by using the price-earnings ratio (PER), which is likely to be more representative than a price-dividend ratio for countries, like China, where dividend distribution is somewhat uneven.

Leaving aside short-lived episodes (shorter than one month, such as late 2006), three main bubble episodes can be identified for the PER of the Shanghai market (Fig. 4.10), with the composite index, over the period since the end of the mid-2000s with weekly data[6] (Girardin et al. 2018).

---

[4] An alternative method for dating bubbles, mainly used by practitioners, relies on the detection of a faster-than-exponential increase in stock prices as the main diagnostic of bubbles. For mainland China this approach detects two bubbles from mid-2005 to October 2007 and from November 2008 to August 2009 (Jiang et al. 2010).

[5] The Phillips et al. (2014, 2015) test has been shown to outperform several other approaches when multiple bubbles occur in the data, and to be easier to implement than regime-switching alternatives.

[6] The 2009 bubble is not apparent in Shanghai's Price-dividend ratio when the dating of bubbles uses monthly data (Liu et al. 2016).

The first of these bubbles, from mid-January to late June, and from early August to early October 2007, came after a very durable bear market which spanned almost the whole first half of the 2000s. This bubble was an immediate by-product of the implementation, late 2006, of the split-share reform, which generated optimistic investor expectations (Li 2015; and Chap. 3). That bubble burst in the early Autumn of 2007, when earnings stopped validating such expectations.

The second bubble, which arose early July and burst in mid-August 2009, marked the end of a long bull market (Jiang et al. 2010). The very short duration of that bubble is rather surprising given the record expansion of bank credit initiated by the Chinese authorities. In a Chinese version of Quantitative Easing directly targeting bank credit, in order to try and counter the economic slowdown associated with the Global Financial Crisis and China's domestic factors, the government (successfully) ordered state-owned banks to lend on a large scale (Deng et al. 2015) in the first semester of 2009. As a result annual credit growth was larger than 30%. However, such credit may have moved rapidly to the real estate market, since a lengthy bubble did start early 2010 in that market, as documented in Deng et al. (2017), who also report evidence of bubble migration from the stock to the housing market.

The third bubble, like the first one, had two components, initially with a short episode spanning the whole December 2014, followed by a much longer one lasting the whole of Spring 2015. This bubble benefited from active stimulation both by the government, talking up the market, and the regulator (the China Securities and Regulatory Commission, CSRC) which relaxed rules on margin trading (introduced in 2010),[7] and lowered collateral requirements. Moreover, monetary easing by the People's Bank of China (PBoC) provided additional macroeconomic liquidity from mid-Autumn 2014. The countervailing actions taken by the CSRC, including a tightening of margin requirements (January and April 2015) and a widening of short-selling to a larger number of stocks, did not prove sufficient to dampen the rise in stock prices. The bubble was pricked mid-June 2015, at the time of the announcement by CSRC of plans aimed at limiting lending for stock trading by brokerages.

---

[7] Over its first five years of existence, margin trading expanded more than five-fold (from US$65 billion).

4.3   Seasonality

Many anomalies characterize the Chinese A-share markets. This includes irregularities—manipulation of prices, underground private investment funds, insider trading and rumour spreading—poor disclosure of information, as well as government interference. Accordingly we expect informational efficiency to be violated due to predictability based for example on seasonal effects.

Efficiency implies that stock returns should not be predictable on the basis of their own past values. In the Chinese A-share market returns do seem to be predictable since over its whole existence (1991–2018) the sum of autoregressive coefficients has been significant (0.16) at the weekly, monthly and quarterly frequencies. Autoregression is still present at the annual frequency. However, given the sharp reversals associated with the burst of bubbles, it is not surprising to find a very sharp negative (-0.42) sum of autoregressive yearly returns.

A major anomaly, neglected by academics, but known to practitioners, is the unusual seasonal behaviour of stock returns in China. Due to major changes in the structural features of China's stock market, involving its regulation as well as the nature and behaviour of investors and the deepening of the market, the seasonal pattern of returns is likely to have changed substantially over time. After a few hectic years in the first half of the 1990s, the implementation of the Company law (July 1994) led to a major improvement in the disclosure of information. Listed firms, in particular, have to produce yearly and mid-year financial statements (Chen et al. 2001). Changes in the late 1990s occurred at the level of regulation, investors, and market. The CSRC enhanced the supervision of, and increased the penalty for, speculators from 2001 onwards. The presence of institutional investors has been noticeable since 1998, with an especially large increase in the number and width of mutual fund companies after 2001, as documented in Chap. 3. Finally, the size of both the listed companies and the market itself increased very fast, making it presumably harder and harder to corner the market.

At low frequencies, some unusual seasonal regularity has been noticed by observers of the Chinese stock market (Girardin and Liu 2003). According to this recurring pattern, stock prices would tend to move up slowly in the first quarter, when speculators accumulate their holdings of stocks. During March and April such speculators would attempt to corner the market and bid up the price. From the end of April, especially after national Labour Day (May 1st), the speculators would try to reduce their holdings when the price is still high. After the middle of June, they would get money back from the sale of their stocks plus a capital gain, and then pay back what they borrowed. Some of them would play the same game from early Autumn, especially around National Day (October 1st). They would sell part of their holdings at such a time, and would get rid of their whole holdings by the end of the year in order to pay back their debts. In some sense, the Chinese market would be a loan-driven speculative market.

To detect the seasonal pattern in stock returns it is necessary to consider capital gains and not dividend-inclusive stock returns. In the Chinese context this is a natural step since, for a substantial period, firms hardly distributed any dividends. However, even for other markets, where firms do distribute regular dividends, some research favours using capital gains data (Pagan and Sossounov 2003). At any rate, in China the volatility of dividend-inclusive returns is similar to that of capital gains since the dividend yield has low variation at high frequencies.

It is common practice to use a smoothing method called CensusX (developed by the US Census Bureau[8]) to detect time-variation in seasonality. The corresponding seasonal factor (logarithm of observed index minus logarithm of seasonally-adjusted index) is plotted in Fig. 4.6 for the Shanghai Composite Index on the last day of every month from January 1991 to October 2018. Since 1993, China's stock exchange has been characterized by two series of regularities concerning respectively the annual highest and lowest returns. The highest returns have moved to an earlier and earlier period during the year. Indeed this maximum, which took place initially in July (from 1993 to 1997), moved in sequence to June (in 1996 and from 1998 to 2001), May (from 2002 to 2007), and April (2008–2017). The lowest (i.e. most negative) returns have also taken place earlier in the year but with some reversion. Indeed, such lowest returns initially corresponded to a December effect (from 1994 to 1997), followed by a dominant October effect (both from 2001 to 2007 and from 2015 to 2017), with two exceptions, a negative Summer effect (from 2010 to 2014) and an earlier negative Winter effect (in 1992–1993 and 1998–2000).[9]

---

[8] https://www.census.gov/srd/www/x13as/x13down_unix.html.

[9] Given the strength of the Red-May effect, Girardin and Liu (2003) make sure that such anomalous returns are not wiped out by seasonal variation in risk, or by news in output growth.

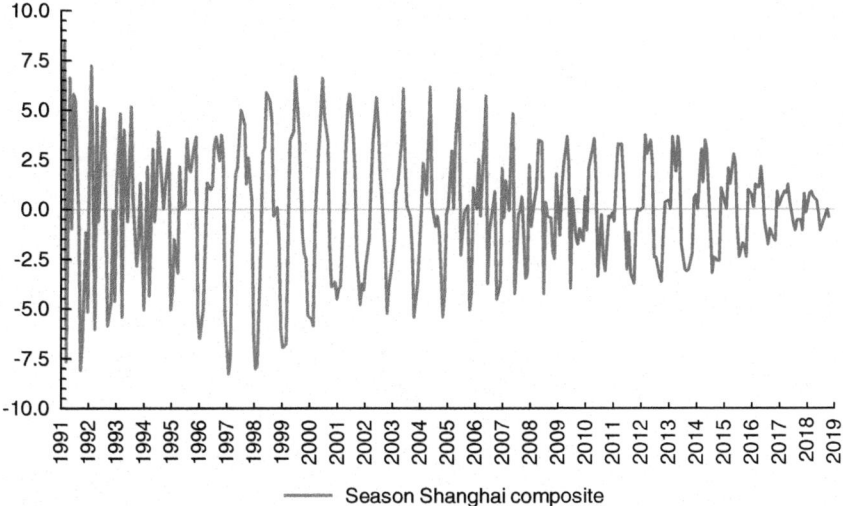

Fig. 4.6 Monthly seasonal factor (%) in Shanghai's composite index: January 1991–October 2018. Note: Time-varying monthly seasonal factor of the Shanghai composite index extracted with CensusX12 (Source: Bloomberg)

The seasonal pattern of the approximation of growth of the manufacturing production volume provided by satellite data (sourced from SpaceKnow, via Bloomberg) has a strong correlation with the seasonal movements of the stock market returns, as shown in Fig. 4.7. During the period 2008–2011, due to the financial crisis of 2008 and the excessively loose credit policy in early 2009, this relationship was somewhat confusing. From 2011 onwards, the stock market and the proxy for industrial production have had the same timing of the lowest points in their seasonal curve. There is some similarity in the seasonal timing of the highest points of the two series, but the degree of coincidence is not as good as for the lowest points.

The seasonality of the stock market and the seasonality of bank credit show a striking similarity in their timing, as shown in Fig. 4.8. This seasonal correlation changes over time, and a lead-lag relationship arises. The highest growth in credit has taken place in June every year since 2000, except over 2005–2007, when it was experienced in April. From 2008 to 2012, persistently high credit growth took place repeatedly from April through June. In 2014–2015 and 2018, the second highest credit growth

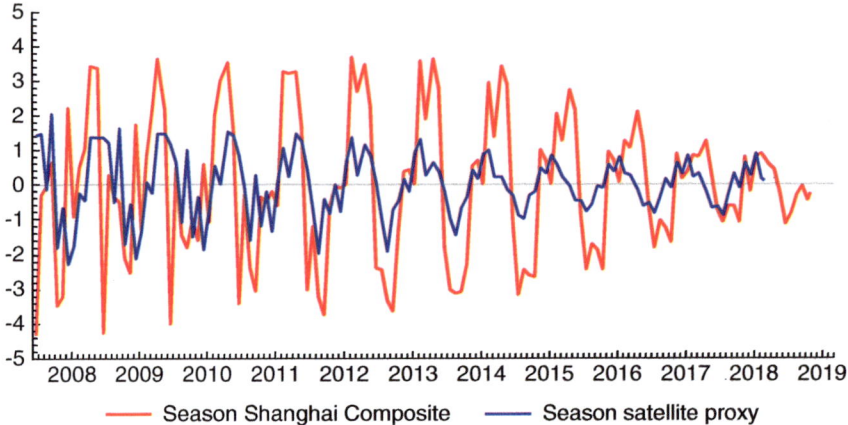

Fig. 4.7 Monthly seasonal factor in Shanghai composite index and satellite proxy for manufacturing output: 2007(6)–2018(2) (%). Note: Time-varying monthly seasonal factor extracted with CensusX12. Shanghai composite index and output and China Satellite manufacturing index (Source: SpaceKnow, via Bloomberg)

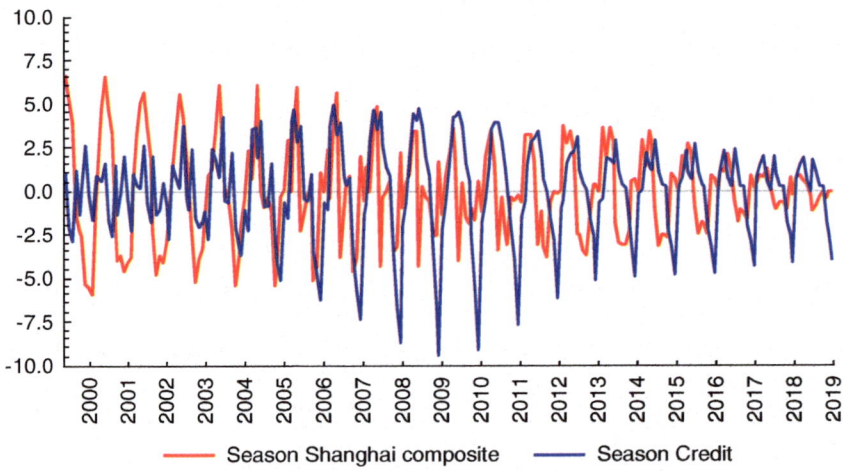

Fig. 4.8 Monthly seasonal factor: Shanghai composite index and bank credit 1999(6)–2018(12) (%). Note: Time-varying monthly seasonal factor extracted with CensusX12. Shanghai composite index (Source: Bloomberg) and bank credit to non-financial sector (Source: BIS and Datastream). For bank credit multiplied by 5

took place in March. The highest return of the stock market and the highest credit growth generally coincide until 2007. From 2008 to 2010 the high credit growth persists for a few months. Over 2011–2014 the highest returns (which are now a little persistent) are slightly leading the highest credit growth, while the pattern is less clear-cut subsequently.

It is customary in China for banks, which decide to award credit lines, to wait until the annual People's congress meeting, usually held in March, which decides the economic and financial policy with the associated annual growth in total bank credit. It is expected that the banks would only partly release some funds in January, and the remaining part would only be released in April or May after the People's Congress. This behavior may be able to explain the seasonal movements in bank credit growth.

Until 2001 there is no overlap between the lowest returns and lowest credit growth, from 2002 to 2005 they coincide, and subsequently the minimum in stock returns always leads the credit growth minimum. It is not surprising that the minimum (with the most negative growth) would be in December for credit growth, as experienced since 2003, in as much as loans have to be paid back at the end of the year. The maturity of the vast majority of the loans from Chinese commercial banks is at most one year. After 2005 there is persistence in peak growth of bank credit, especially in 2008–2010, which may have led investors to take positions in 2011–2014, in order to try and profit from the seasonal credit growth pattern that they experienced from the crisis onwards. Unfortunately for these investors, the persistence in the seasonal peak in credit growth did not repeat itself. A full study of such seasonal patterns and relationships would require the use of rigorous and complex methodology, which lies outside the scope of this work.

4.4   An Alphabet Soup of Premia

Segmentation has been a major feature of China's stock markets. This market has been divided from its very beginning between multiple venues. The resulting alphabet soup of price-premia has long puzzled may observers. The Shanghai and Shenzhen stock markets were designed initially as segmented between a large and dominant component, the A-market, denominated in Chinese Renminbi, reserved to domestic investors, and the B-market, denominated in foreign currency, initially restricted to foreign investors. Due to highly-binding capital controls, the multiple listing of Chinese firms on both domestic and foreign stock exchanges has resulted in some further premia. The main premium has been with the Hong Kong stock market, where the index of mainland firms, so-called H-shares, dominated in Hong Kong dollars, represents a dominant part of the Hang-Seng index.

4.4.1   From Trade to Financial Openness

Existing theoretical work provides rationales and empirical work supporting evidence (surveyed in Girardin and Liu 2003) that external *de jure* financial openness is neither a sufficient nor a necessary condition for foreign stock prices to influence domestic stock prices. On the theoretical side, with high trade openness, *de jure* protection of a domestic financial market, through capital controls, does not prevent *de facto* financial openness (Aizenman 2003). On a descriptive side, using measures of *de facto* financial openness based on gross capital flows as a share of GDP, China appears as an example of a "group of countries [for which] gross inflows and gross outflows have both been large and roughly similar in magnitude, reflecting increased financial integration with the world economy" (Lane and Milesi-Feretti 2005). China has experienced large capital inflows, mainly through FDI, and outflows, but also significant net foreign asset accumulation, mostly as foreign exchange reserves. Overall, potential channels for hidden capital flows to and from China are important.[10]

4.4.2   A and B Markets

Despite their identical rights, measured in the same currency, the prices of A-shares were on average four times higher than the prices of corresponding B-shares during the first ten years of the market, in the 1990s. Such a B-shares discount relative to A-share prices presented a puzzle to observers, as foreign investors should be able to diversify country risk, leading B-shares to trade at a premium, in line with what is observed in other countries with similar arrangements (Bailey et al. 1999).

It is worth mentioning here the principal steps in the regulatory reform in the B market, since the relationship with the A market should be con-

---

[10] The evidence on the huge scale of round-tripping behind foreign direct investment, which, according to Xiao (2004), had a mean value of 40% of recorded FDI, shows that such hidden flows do take place on a large scale.

sidered within each of those stages. There is a presumption that such a relationship would have been strongly affected by the regulatory changes.

In early 1992 Chinese authorities decided to create the B-share market, in order to lure foreign investors, portraying the A and B segments as the two wings enabling the stock market to fly. Such a combination was certainly ideally suited to the conditions prevailing at the time, involving in particular tight capital controls, and a still low degree of trade openness.

On June 28, 1996, the CSRC issued a new announcement to regulate the B-share investors, which implied that only foreign investors would be allowed to hold B-shares. On September 20th the same year CSRC decided to close all unqualified B-share accounts, and reserve this market strictly to investors from Greater China (HK, Macao, and Taiwan) and Chinese citizens holding permanent resident status abroad.

On February 24, 1998, the Securities Committee of the State Council released a 'new regulation on B-share company follow-up public offering', accepting for the first time that B-share companies fulfilling the requirements would be allowed to do their Seasoned equity offerings, and on July 11, 1998, CSRC relaxed auditing requirements on B-shares.

Due to the surge in IPOs by mainland companies on the Hong Kong stock market in 1997, the B-share market lost its attractiveness for foreign investors. Several factors led to such a drop in the appeal to investors, such as the small market size, the poor quality of information disclosure as well as the low profits of firms listed in the B-markets. Accordingly, international investors turned away from the B-markets, which started to hibernate. Up to 1999 only one out of the ten formerly most important investors remained on the B-share markets.

On February 19, 2001, the CSRC opened the B-share markets also to domestic investors. The objective of the authorities thus shifted from attracting international investors to this market to wooing domestic investors holding foreign currencies. With little consideration for risk, such domestic investors started speculating in the B-share markets. This new policy implied that domestic investors, when buying B-shares, had to use foreign currency deposited, prior to that date, with Chinese banks. On June 1, 2001 such a time restriction was lifted but the requirement of a prior holding of foreign currency deposits was retained.

As of December 2003, 111 companies had issued a total of 19 billion B-shares, raising 35.6 billion RMB. As of the same date, 1287 companies were listed, of which 1146 issued A-shares only, 24 issued B-shares only, 87 issued both A-shares and B-shares, and 30 issued both A- and H-shares.

During the whole active period of the B market in the 1990s, this market was trading at a discount with respect to the A market. Diverse explanations of such a discount have been put forward. This included a potential information advantage of domestic investors and the relative illiquidity of the B-share market (Chakravarty et al. 1998; Karolyi and Li 2003; Chan and Kwok 2005). A third explanation motivates the A-B share-premium by investors' speculative motive. On a panel of 73 Chinese double-listed stocks in the A and B segments over 1993–2001, there is evidence that shares with larger overvaluation also have a larger turnover (Mei et al. 2009). Trading generated by the speculative motive explains one-fifth of the cross-sectional variation in the B-share discount up to December 2000. During the year following its opening to domestic investors the B-share market saw a sharp rise in both prices and turnover, implying that speculation by domestic investors may have started to affect that market.

Existing empirical work (reviewed in Girardin and Liu 2009) focused almost exclusively on the period before the 2001 reform. However, such a reform, allowing Chinese residents, in particular, to operate in the B-market, should have represented a watershed in the relationships between A- and B-share market prices, due to the novel arbitrage by domestic investors. However, a study of the different steps in the development of the regulation of the B-share market casts doubts on the relevance of such a focus on the 2001 reform (Girardin and Liu 2009). Just as important as the reform at the turn of the new millennium were the major changes which took place in two major steps in 1996 and 1998, which we have just reviewed. The movements of the B-shares market vis-a-vis the A-shares market do reflect such changes in regulation (Fig. 4.9). Indeed, until 1996 there is at times some relationship between the two markets. By contrast, over the 1996–1998 period, the B-shares market disconnects itself sharply from the A-shares market, the latter remaining stable, while the former falls. Between 1998 and 2001, the two markets disconnect from each other, and subsequently reconnect. Indeed, after 2001 the B-shares market follows the A market in its bearish phase and, after late 2005, in its bullish phase, as well as in the speculative episode of 2007–2008. Over the last decade the B-shares market has mimicked movements in the A market.

More formal tests vindicate this descriptive analysis. Indeed, the main message from both adjusted correlations and adjusted betas[11] is that the

---

[11] To compare correlations across markets between two time periods, they are corrected for changes in variance. The betas between the two markets are corrected in a similar way.

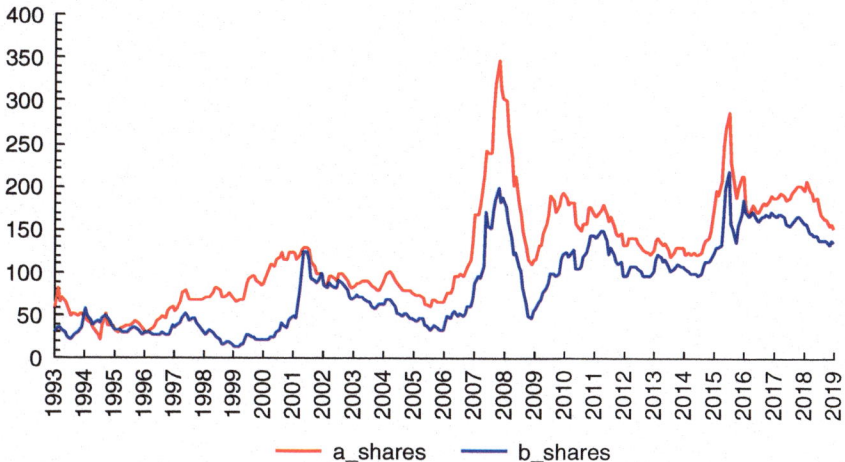

Fig. 4.9 A- and B-share indices in Shanghai. Monthly data 1993(1)–2018(12). The base is 2001(12) = 100. A and B indices in RMB (Source: Wind)

major break in the relationship between the A- and B-share markets happened in 1998 and not in 2001 (Girardin and Liu 2003). The beta of the B-shares market returns vis-a-vis the A-shares market returns has been very close to one since 1998. After 2004, in the absence of new IPOs on the B-shares market, and with the latter fully emulating movements in the A-shares market, it is arguable that the discontinuation of the B-shares market would not have been costly in net terms. The benefits of its presence may not have outweighed its costs (including supervision). This was all the more so given the gradual external opening of the A-share market via the Qualified Foreign Institutional Investors (QFII) and the subsequent Stock Connect schemes, reviewed in Chap. 3.

4.4.3 A and H Markets and Capital Controls

Intermarket price arbitrage should be expected between dual-listed shares on the mainland and Hong Kong markets. It is useful to distinguish between two types of direct price arbitrage (Deardorff 1979): the trading of an asset with different prices across markets (pure arbitrage), and moving away from an asset to invest in another one with higher expected return but the same risk (quasi arbitrage). Quasi arbitrage is at work, for example, when an investor in the domestic market sells (buys) a dual-listed stock when the price (returns) of the stock in that market is higher (lower) than that (those) in the corresponding foreign market. Pure arbitrage of dual-listed stocks requires much stricter conditions, that is, that both the currency and stock markets can be accessed freely, that there is no exchange control, no restriction on capital flows, and synchronous cross-market settlement. Quasi arbitrage is able to generate co-movements in prices but not necessarily price convergence, while such convergence can be generated by pure arbitrage in a perfect market setting (Fung et al. 2016; Peng et al. 2007).

A rigid dollar peg for the Chinese RMB was in force until late July 2005, again from July 2008 to June 2010, and a de facto (crawling) peg was enforced subsequently, at least until 2015 (Girardin and Salimi Namin 2018), while the Hong Kong dollar has been in a currency board regime with the US dollar for three-and-a-half decades. Before the late 2014 Stock Connect, mainland investors were prohibited by law to trade stocks listed in Hong Kong (or other overseas markets) with their stock accounts in the mainland, while Hong Kong or other foreign investors could not trade the A-shares listed on both mainland exchanges. Further, mainlanders are prohibited from remitting money abroad (over some low threshold, 50 thousand US$ per year since 2007) and overseas investors, including those in Hong Kong, cannot directly transfer money to a bank account in the mainland.

Existing evidence for dual-listed stocks in different segmented markets for most countries (as diverse as Mexico, Indonesia, Malaysia, Norway, Singapore, Switzerland, and Thailand; see review in Fung et al. 2016) supports the presence of a premium on foreign-listed shares over domestic ones. In a somewhat puzzling way (Fernald and Rogers 2006), for Chinese dual-listed shares, the opposite has been documented: Chinese A-shares have enjoyed a premium over the same mainland companies' H-shares listed in Hong Kong, when measured in the same currency. Diverse specificities of China's setting have been proposed to explain this puzzle, such as: information asymmetries between domestic and foreign investors; differences in liquidity conditions; a speculative motive of domestic investors; differential risk; differing market conditions; and short-sale restrictions (fully binding until the late 2000s).

The respective role of such factors is examined by Fung et al. (2016) for 26 dual-listed firms in the A-share and H-share markets over the period 2004–2009, with aggregated intraday data, averaged over the daily two hours of overlapping trading sessions of the two markets. Their cross-sectional study generates three main results. First, the switch to a managed-floating exchange-rate regime of July 2005 is associated with an increase rather than a decrease in the H-share discount. Second, information asymmetry contributes to explaining the fall in the cross-sectional variation of the H-share discount only before mid-2005, but not thereafter; which could be due to the 2005 split-share reform alongside the switch to floating. Third, after that same date, speculative trading has the largest impact on the H-share discount. In addition, with a panel-data analysis, Fung et al. (2016) show that an expected appreciation of the RMB has an asymmetric effect under fixed and floating exchange rates: it decreases (increases) the H-share discount in the fixed (flexible) exchange-rate regime period. Besides, the (initial) prohibition of short-selling in A-shares appears to be a reason why the H-share discount rises when the market goes down.

The absence of a long-run link between the Chinese and foreign stock markets has often been interpreted as proof of the lack of international financial integration of China.[12] Care should be taken in drawing such an inference since tests of long-run relationships per se may not be informative with respect to market integration (Lence and Falk 2005). Asset prices are ultimately determined by the relevant endowment processes. Such prices will entertain a long-run relationship (i.e. be co-integrated), or not, depending on the similarities of endowment processes, not on market integration. The evidence with regards to the relationship between markets in Shanghai and Hong Kong cannot be questioned on the basis of such a distinction since fundamentals are simply the same due to the dual-listing of mainland firms in both markets. In other words, stock prices differ significantly between Shanghai and Hong Kong (in its H-share segment) even for the same firms.

Figure 4.10 shows PERs in the Shanghai composite and the Hong Kong H-shares exchanges. The two PERs converged only very temporarily in the Autumn of 2008, after Lehman's bankruptcy. Among the three major bubbles experienced by the Shanghai market in less than a decade after the mid-2000s, the Hong Kong market only experienced the first one, in 2007 (see the dating of explosive PER periods for both markets presented by Girardin et al. 2018). Indeed, bubble-migration tests imply

---

[12] Many empirical studies of financial integration have examined the case of China, always with daily data (Girardin and Liu 2007, for a survey of early work).

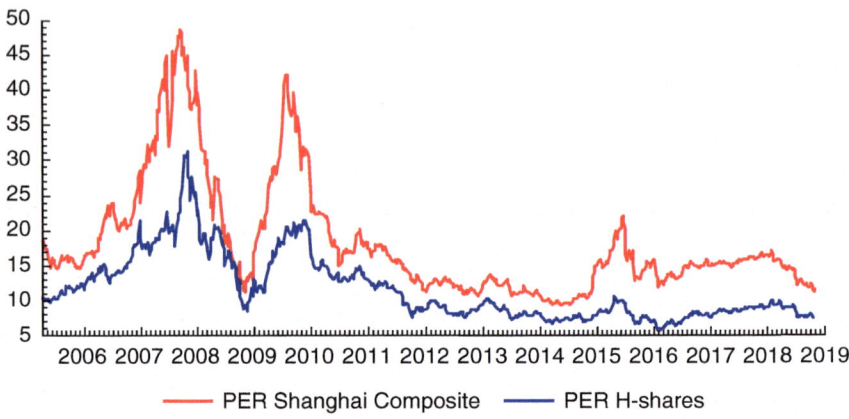

Fig. 4.10 Price-earnings ratios in Shanghai's Composite Index and Hong Kong H-shares. Price-earnings ratio (PER) Shanghai composite and Hong Kong H-shares: Weekly data April 2005–October 2018 (Source: Bloomberg)

that, only during the latter episode, evidence can be gathered of migration of the Shanghai bubble to the H-share and Hang Seng indices. The bubbles in Hong Kong only started when the Shanghai one was in its dying stage. There is thus no evidence that the 2014 Stock Connect subsequently led in any way to bubble transmission from Shanghai to Hong Kong, or of bubble mitigation in the mainland by North-bound flows.

The correlation with global markets is a major concern for international investors, eager to access China's stock market, especially with the gradual opening associated with the qualified investor schemes and recently with the Stock Connects (See Chap. 3 and Kashyap 2016). The relationship between returns in the Chinese and the US stock markets has sharply increased over time. Indeed the beta coefficient representing the link of Chinese returns with US returns, which was insignificant in the 1990s and before the global crisis (Table 4.2), became significant thereafter and close to one after the start of the Stock Connect. Benefits of diversification for foreign investors in the Chinese market can be inferred from its low correlation coefficient with the US market which has only become substantial since the global crisis, and risen since the Stock Connect, but is still much below one.

Over and above summary measures provided by correlations, the links between China's and the US market can be assessed by focusing on the

Table 4.2   The effect of US stock returns on China's stock returns

	Beta	*Correlation*
1991(1)–1999(12)	−0.05	−0.003
2000(1)–2008(8)	0.122	0.076
2008(9)–2014(10)	0.427***	0.195***
2014(11)–2018(10)	1.06***	0.512***

The beta coefficient is estimated by regressing the monthly (last day of month) returns in the Chinese stock market (Δy) on its own first lag and on the S&P500 monthly (last but one day of month) returns (Δx), as $\Delta y_t = \alpha + \beta \, \Delta x_t + \chi \, \Delta y_{t-1} + \varepsilon_t$. Ordinary Least Squares. ***Significant at the 1% level (standard errors are adjusted for autocorrelation and heteroscedasticity). Shanghai A-share index (Source: Bloomberg) and S&P500 (Source: Saint Louis Federal Reserve Bank)

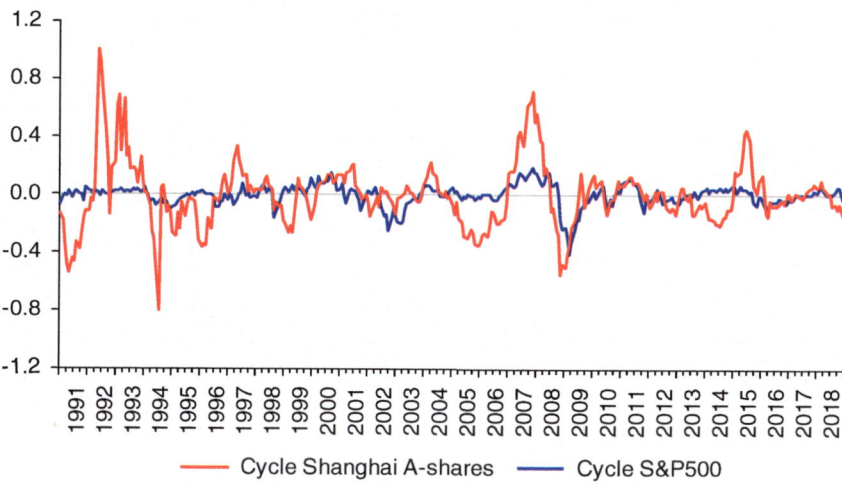

Fig. 4.11   Cyclical components of S&P500 and Shanghai A-shares indices: 1991(2)–2018(12). Cyclical component extracted with a Hodrick–Prescott filter (Lambda equals 14,400) for the Shanghai A-share index (Source: Bloomberg) and the Standard and Poor's index (Source: Federal Reserve bank of St. Louis). Data on the last day of every month for Shanghai, and on the last but one day for New York

correspondence between their cyclical movements, which can separate bull from bear markets. Before the global financial crisis of 2008 such links do not seem to be present, with the possible exception of the early millennium (Fig. 4.11). Such links would have vanished from 2013 to 2015, and reappeared subsequently.

4.5   SUMMARY AND CONCLUSIONS

Due to its design and organization, the Chinese stock market combines most of the features which are known to make a stock exchange inherently speculative. In particular listed firms do not regularly pay dividends, which compels (often immature) investors to rely only on expected capital gains. As a result, stock prices, outside their lasting bear phases, either skyrocket or plummet, sharply diverging from earnings. Even after the split-share reform of the mid-2000s, the Chinese stock market experienced three major bubbles: in 2007, in July–August 2009, and in late Autumn 2014 and Spring 2015. The rise and burst of the most recent of these bubbles were mostly related to government involvement.

Seasonality in the Chinese stock market pertains to a 'Spring and Autumn' pattern. Indeed, differently from western markets, in China the seasonal anomaly of high monthly positive returns is not identified with a January effect but with a unique 'Red May Effect', and the lowest returns do not take place in December but in October. Of course, with the continuous improvement of China's stock market regulation and supervision, the growing market size, the gradual learning by investors and structural changes, this seasonal pattern has also undergone some changes over time, but the main regularity remains. The seasonal pattern of China's stock market has a high similarity both with the seasonality of the proxy of gross industrial output derived from satellite data, and the seasonality of bank loans.

Due to the control of the capital account and historical reasons, the Chinese stock market has been divided into the A-share market for domestic investors and the B-share market for foreign investors. Moreover, the widespread listing of mainland firms in Hong Kong has given rise to a specific type of share, H-shares. This makes the Chinese stock market look like an alphabet soup, and has created puzzles, since premia between these different exchanges listing the same companies' shares are usually opposite to what they are for other countries' firms in other markets. The segmentation initially facilitated the development of China's stock market, but also raised difficulties for subsequent capital account reforms and stock market opening.

REFERENCES

Aizenman, J. 2003. On the Hidden Links Between Financial and Trade Opening. NBER Working Paper 9906.

Allen, F, J. Qian, S.C. Shan, and J.L. Zhu. 2014. The Best Performing Economy with the Worst Performing Stock Market: Explaining the Poor Performance of the Chinese Stock Market, Manuscript, Imperial College, University of London.

Bailey, W., P. Chung, and J.-K. Kang. 1999. Foreign Ownership Restrictions and Equity Price Premiums: What Drives the Demand for Cross-border Investments? *Journal of Financial and Quantitative Analysis* 34: 489–512.

Binde, P. 2005. Gambling Across Cultures: Mapping Worldwide Occurrence and Learning from Ethnographic Comparison. *International Gambling Studies* 5 (1): 1–27.

de Bondt, G.J., T.A. Peltonen, and D. Santabárbara. 2010. Booms and Busts in China's Stock Market: Estimates Based on Fundamentals. ECB Working Paper, No. 1190.

Chakravarty, S., A. Sarkar, and L. Wu. 1998. Information Asymmetry, Market Segmentation and the Pricing of Cross-listed Shares: Theory and Evidence from Chinese A and B Shares. Working Paper, Federal Reserve Bank of New York, Research Department.

Chan, K., and J.K. Kwok. 2005. Market Segmentation and Share Price Premium: Evidence from Chinese Stock Markets. *Journal of Emerging Market Finance* 4: 43–61.

Chen, G., C.C.Y. Kwok, and O.M. Rui. 2001. The Day-of-the-Week Regularity in the Stock Markets of China. *Journal of Mathematical Financial Management* 11: 139–163.

Chi, W., R. Brooks, E. Bissoondoyal-Bheenick, and X. Tang. 2016. Classifying Chinese Bull and Bear Market: Indices and Individual Stocks. *Studies in Economics and Finance* 33 (4): 509–531.

Deardorff, A.V. 1979. One-way Arbitrage, and Its Implications for the Foreign Exchange Market. *Journal of Political Economy* 87 (2): 351–364.

Deng, Y., E. Girardin, R. Joyeux, and S. Shi. 2017. Did Bubbles Migrate from the Stock to the Housing Market in China from 2005 to 2010? *Pacific Economic Review* 22 (3): 276–292.

Deng, Y., R. Morck, J. Wu, and B. Yeung. 2015. China's Pseudo-monetary Policy. *Review of Finance* 19: 55–93.

Diba, B.T., and H.I. Grossman. 1988. Explosive Rational Bubbles in Stock Prices? *American Economic Review* 78 (3): 520–530.

Fama, E. 1970. Efficient Capital Markets: A Review of Theory and Empirical Work. *Journal of Finance* 25 (2): 383–417.

Fernald, J., and J.H. Rogers. 2006. Puzzle Sin the Chinese Stock Market. *Review of Economics and Statistics* 84 (3): 416–432.

Fung, J., E. Girardin, and J. Hua. 2016. How does an Exchange-rate Regime Change Affect Dual-listed Stock Arbitrage? Evidence from China's A- and H-share Markets, Manuscript, Aix Marseille School of Economics, Aix Marseille University.

Girardin, E., and F. Salimi Namin. 2018. *Shadowing the Dollar or Basket Pegging in China?* Aix Marseille School of Economics, February, Manuscript.

Girardin, E., and R. Joyeux. 2013. Macro Fundamentals as a Source of Stock Market Volatility in China: A GARCH-MIDAS Approach. *Economic Modelling* 34: 59–68.

Girardin, E., R. Joyeux, and S. Shi. 2018. Stock Market Bubble Migration: From Shanghai to Hong Kong. In *Uncertainty, Expectations and Asset Price Dynamics*, ed. F. Jawadi, 173–192. Springer.

Girardin, E., and Z. Liu. 2003. The Chinese Stock Market: A Casino with Buffer Zones. *Journal of Chinese Economic and Business Studies* 1 (1): 57–70.

———. 2005. Bank Credit and Seasonal Anomalies in China's Stock Markets. *China Economic Review* 16 (4): 465–483.

———. 2007. The Financial Integration of China: New Evidence on Temporally Aggregated Data for the A-share Market. *China Economic Review* 18: 354–371.

———. 2009. Is the B-share Market Ripe for Merging with the A-market or was it Already Long Ago? *Journal of Renmin University of China* 4 (1): 11–24.

Groenewold, N.S., Y. Wu, H.K. Tanang, and X.M. Fan. 2004. *The Chinese Stock Market: Efficiency, Predictability and Profitability*. Cheltenham: Edward Elgar.

Guo, K., Y. Sun, and X. Qian. 2017. Can investor Sentiment be Used to Predict the Stock Price? Dynamic Analysis based on China Stock Market. *Physica A* 469: 390–396.

Han, X., and Y. Li. 2017. Can Investor Sentiment be a Momentum Time-series Predictor? *Journal of Empirical Finance* 42: 212–239.

Harman, Y.S., and T.W. Zuehlke. 2004. Duration Dependence Testing for Speculative Bubbles. *Journal of Economics and Finance* 28 (2): 147–154.

Hodrick, R., and E. Prescott. 1997. Postwar US Business Cycles: An Empirical Investigation. *Journal of Money, Credit and Banking* 29 (1): 1–16.

Hong, H., J. Scheinkman, and W. Xiong. 2006. Asset Float and Speculative Bubbles. *Journal of Finance* 61: 1073–1117.

Jiang, Z., W. Zhou, D. Sornette, R. Woodard, K. Bastiaensen, and P. Cauwels. 2010. Bubble Diagnosis and Prediction of the 2005–2007 and 2008–2009 Chinese Stock Market Bubbles. *Journal of Economic Behavior and Organization* 74: 149–162.

Kang, J., M.H. Liu, and S.X. Ni. 2002. Contrarian and Momentum Strategies in the China Stock Market: 1993–2000. *Pacific basin Finance Journal* 10 (3): 243–265.

Karolyi, G.A., and Li, L. 2003. A Resolution of the Chinese Discount Puzzle. Dice Center Working Paper 2003/34.

Kashyap, R. 2016. Hong Kong-Shanghai Connect/Hong Kong-Beijing Disconnect? Scaling the Great Wall of Chinese Securities Trading Costs. *Journal of Trading* 11 (3): 81–134.

Lane, P.R., and G.-M. Milesi-Feretti. 2005. Financial Globalization and Exchange Rates. Working Paper 05/3, International Monetary Fund.

Lence, S., and B. Falk. 2005. Cointegration, Market Integration, and Market Efficiency. *Journal of International Money and Finance* 24: 873–890.

Li, Z. 2015. Emergence of China's 2006–2007 Stock Market Bubble and Its Burst. In *The Chinese Stock Market*, ed. S. Cheng and Z. Li, vol. 2, 61–124. Basingstoke: Palgrave Macmillan.

Li, C.-A., and C.-C. Yeh. 2011. Investor Psychological and Behavioural Biases: Do High Sentiment and Momentum Exist in the China Stock Market? *Review of Pacific Basin Financial Markets and Policies* 14 (3): 429–448.

Liu, Z., D. Han, and S. Wang. 2016. Testing Bubbles: Exuberance and Collapse in Shanghai A-share Market. In *China's New Sources of Economic Growth, Vol. 1. Reform, Resources and Climate Change*, ed. L. Song, R. Garnaut, C. Fang, and L. Johnston, 247–270. Acton: Australian National University Press.

Malkiel, B.G. 2007. The Efficiency of the Chinese Stock Market: Some Unfinished Business on the Road to Economic Transformation. CEPS Working Paper, 154.

McQueen, G., and S. Thorley. 1994. Bubbles, Stock Returns, and Duration Dependence. *Journal of Financial and Quantitative Analysis* 29 (3): 379–401.

Mei, J., J. Scheinkman, and W. Xiong. 2009. Speculative Trading and Stock Prices: An Analysis of Chinese A-B Share Premia. *Annals of Economics and Finance* 10: 225–255.

Ni, Z.-X., D.-Z. Wang, and W.-J. Xue. 2015. Investor Sentiment and Its Non-linear Effect on Stock Returns: New Evidence from the Chinese Stock Market Based on Panel Quantile Regression Model. *Economic Modelling* 50: 266–274.

Pagan, A.R., and K.A. Sossounov. 2003. A Simple Framework for Analysing Bull and Bear Markets. *Journal of Applied Econometrics* 18 (1): 23–46.

Peng, W., H. Miao, and N. Chow. 2007. Macroeconomic Linkages between Hong Kong and Mainland China. Working Paper 6/07, Hong Kong Monetary Authority.

Phillips, P.C., S. Shi, and J. Yu. 2014. Specification Sensitivity in Right-tailed Unit-root Testing for Explosive Behaviour. *Oxford Bulletin of Economics and Statistics* 76 (3): 315–333.

Phillips, P.C.B., S. Shi, and J. Yu. 2015. Testing for Multiple Bubbles: Historical Episodes of Exuberance and Collapse in the S&P 500. *International Economic Review* 56: 1043–1078.

Scheinkman, J., and W. Xiong. 2003. Overconfidence and Speculative Bubbles. *Journal of Political Economy* 111: 1183–1219.

Scherbina, A., and B. Schlusche. 2014. Asset Price Bubbles: A Survey. *Quantitative Finance* 14 (4): 589–604.

Sharif, S. 2013. Essays on Short Selling and Margin Trading in China. PhD Thesis, Massey University, New Zealand.

Shiller, R. 1981. Do Stock Prices Move Too Much to Be Justified by Subsequent Changes in Dividends? *American Economic Review* 71: 421–435.

Siegel, J. 2014. *Stocks for the Long Run: The Definitive Guide to Financial Market Returns and Long-term Investment Strategy*. New York: McGraw-Hill.

Wu, H. 2011. The Real Growth of Chinese Industry Debate Revisited: Reconstructing China's Industrial GDP in 1949–2008, Institute of Economic Research, Hitotsubashi University. *Economic Review* 62 (3): 209–224.

Xiao, G. 2004. Roundtripping Foreign Direct Investment and the People's Republic of China. ADBI Working Paper, No. 58, July.

Zhou, Z. 2015. Development and Problems of Stock Index Futures and Margin Trading and Short Selling in China. In *The Chinese Stock Market*, ed. S. Cheng and Z. Li, vol. 1, 313–367. Basingstoke: Palgrave Macmillan.

CHAPTER 5

The Political Economy of an Incomplete Market

Abstract The apparent convergence of the legal framework to international standards may hide major specificities of China's stock market. In spite of the official progress made in creating rules and regulations, the practice of corporate governance is hampered because they are not properly enforced. The multiplicity of principals at work in the pre- and post-initial public offering process reflects core features of the organization of China's state-owned enterprise sector and institutional apparatus. We will analyze these features using a political economy perspective.

The incompleteness of the Chinese stock market is the natural product of government dominance. The Chinese government did not intend to build a complete stock market providing signals for an efficient allocation of capital. The government has always intended to use the stock market as an economic instrument, and to try to keep everything under control. The government does not want the market to provide signals for the allocation of capital because it feels able to provide better signals than those provided by the market. The stock market in China is a politico-economic instrument, not a standard market.

Keywords Political economy • Incomplete market • Corporate governance • Multiple principals • Deconcentration

© The Author(s) 2019   93
E. Girardin, Z. Liu, *Demystifying China's Stock Market*,
https://doi.org/10.1007/978-3-030-17123-0_5

5.1   Introduction

According to Wong (2016): "Scholars often begin and end their analyses by benchmarking the governance attributes of Chinese listed companies against global (which typically means US) corporate governance standards and institutions. This approach…invariably focuses the analyst's attention on what the Chinese system *lacks*, not on how it is constructed and actually functions…Real headway in understanding China's variety of capitalism will come by analysing the system on its own terms rather than principally by reference to something it is not".

This chapter will show that the Chinese stock market departs in many ways from the typical template of markets that one finds in advanced countries. Stocks do not provide a right of ownership over the concerned (especially large listed) state-owned enterprises (SOEs), because private investors remain minority shareholders. Dividend distribution has not provided a regular income on shares. Earnings have been distorted by the high interest rates charged by state-owned banks for loans, and firms often massage their earnings prior to (or even after) listing, disconnecting stock prices from reported earnings.

The limits of China's legal system for the capital market show not so much in the regulations themselves, but in the practice and (lack of) enforcement of the law. For instance, insider trading, while prohibited, is not seriously punished. Information disclosure problems include fake contracts and fake profits.

Large SOEs are almost fully controlled by the government (through the Supervision and Administration Commission of the State Council, SASAC), and shares owned by the state have not been used to regulate the market. The state appoints managers and influences decision-making of SOEs, and, even in the private sector, the interest of small individual investors, or minority shareholders, is not well protected.

Some western research considers that China's stock market is now able to value a listed company, in an appropriate way (Carpenter et al. 2015). However, such an optimistic assessment may be a little premature since the share price generally does not provide the right signals, and the link with the real economy has not been direct. The pricing of initial public offerings (IPOs) favours speculation. Delisting is extremely difficult even in the face of persistent losses. Earnings are often not representative of the profits. This is yet another reason why the firms do not distribute dividends regularly. The profits may be used to finance other (social) activities. Tunnelling can take the form of outsourcing at inflated costs inside the group, via transfer pricing, similar to what takes place inside the *Kereitsus* in Japan (such as Toshiba) or the *Chaebols* in Korea, but in an even more systematic way. SOEs are organized as groups in which the listed company is only a subsidiary and its profits can thus easily be siphoned off by the mother group. This behaviour provides a bad example for private listed companies where large shareholders can also easily capture the profits of their listed subsidiary. Private large shareholders fight to be in control and appoint the managers (as in the Vanke group in 2017).

The multi-layered character of the organization of China's stock market, in particular the multiple principals involved, introduces some de facto competition among those principals along vertical as well as horizontal hierarchies. Furthermore, this is a source of checks and balances on the listing and the price regulation processes, due to a divergence between the various interests at stake. These features can also help reduce social externalities, since there must be some limit to the number of companies listed, otherwise among them too many would fail, given the distortions and immaturity of the infrastructure and of some of the players involved.

5.2   Corporate Governance Chinese Style

The most frequent assessment of the performance of China's stock markets is rather negative (Allen and Shen 2011). Prices would not be efficiently set by the market and governance standards of the legal system they incorporate would be ineffective. As a result, market prices would be able to provide neither a positive signalling (i.e. allocative), nor a disciplinary function in order to ensure a proper corporate management of listed firms. Corporate governance challenges for listed firms, including state intervention, opaque accounting, and expropriation by controlling shareholders (Wong 2016), would contribute to the poor performance of China's stock market (Allen et al. 2014).

The 'law and finance' school[1] stresses the legal protection of shareholders as a requirement for a proper stock market development and

---

[1] China's stock market is often cited as a counterexample to the significance of law for financial development. The trajectory of development in China is growth first followed by law, and the improvement of law is caused by market growth. The experience of China suggests that law and market growth exhibit a bi-directional rather than a uni-directional causal relationship, and the course of development is "growth-law-further growth" (Zhang 2016). See also Chen (2003).

functioning. By contrast, a different perspective considers that the weak legal protection of shareholders on China's stock market did not preclude the very fast expansion of the market (Allen et al. 2005; Pistor and Xu 2005).

On the face of it, China's company law (*Gongsi Fa*) shows remarkable convergence to the standard model of corporate governance, including: limited liability; legal personality; transferable shares; centralized management under a board structure; and shared ownership by providers of capital. These signs of convergence have led many scholars, practitioners, and international organizations to believe that corporate governance in Chinese companies can be understood and analyzed along the lines of the separation of ownership and control (Wang 2014). Most corporate governance scholars working on China have taken the individual firm, the publicly listed company, as the unit of analysis, even though corporate groups are pervasive in the state-owned sector and the listed firm is just one part of a complex web of corporate entities and relationships (Li and Milhaupt 2013).

If the underlying purpose of the state is to control SOEs as tightly as possible, one may wonder why the state did promulgate, and partly enforce, so many national laws, regulations and rules to limit external interference in enterprise management and governance (Wang 2014). The presence of a 'dual governance structure' for SOEs, composed of a structure for legal governance and another one for political governance, is part of the answer.

The reason for a firm in China to adopt a governance system[2] which differs strongly from Western standards is not necessarily due to opportunistic behaviour by managers of firms but can be an optimal response to the key institutional context in which the firm operates. It is important to remember the view of scholars in Chinese law who emphasize that "although, on paper, China has all the apparatus of a western legal system, it is a country that is still heavily influenced by tradition...Traces of the legal system perfected in the Tang dynasty...are very much with us" (Jones 2003, p. 8).

The major issue in China has been enforcement rather than rules or regulation themselves. Concentration of ownership has plagued both state- and privately-owned firms. Decentralized competition for listing within a quota system has often been viewed as a way to fill the governance vacuum. A Chinese-style corporate governance system has gradually

---

[2] A survey and evaluation of corporate governance is provided by Weian and Chen (2015).

evolved in which the multiplicity of principals at both the central and local levels has proved a dominant feature.

5.2.1 Enforcement

Agency theory focuses on the ways to enforce financial contracts between external investors and corporate controllers. Attention is refocused away from substantive laws to enforcement. Alternative institutions, such as stock exchanges, investment banks, or trust in the local business community, can facilitate the growth of stock markets in the absence of legal protection (Coffee 2001; Cheffins 2003). The enforcement school argues that no enforcement mechanism is effective in China. Both state ownership and centralization have severely hampered enforcement mechanisms (Chen 2013a).

As an enforcement mechanism, overseas multiple-listing has not proved very effective. Cross-listing did not change incentives of controllers, due to four reasons (Chen 2013a). First, the costs of cross-listing are not borne by controllers but by Chinese taxpayers. Dividends awarded to investors in foreign-listed mainland firms appear generous, often allowing foreign investors to share in the monopoly rents of Chinese firms which are dominant in their home market. Second, foreign cross-listing does not enable SOEs to resist government intervention and does not alter their soft budget constraint or their multitask character (Chap. 3). Third, cross-listing has limited impact on insider control, and is unable to affect the personnel decision of management, or to prevent possible malfeasance by corporate insiders. Finally, extraterritorial law enforcement faces serious limits. Indeed, exchanges and domestic laws would very often have different rules for foreign firms; international stock exchanges in mutual competition may be unwilling to enforce; and it is doubtful that foreign authorities would be able to act against a Chinese parent company.

As an enforcement mechanism, the provision of assets or equipment as collateral is not prevalent when listed companies receive bank loans, and, even when they are provided, such collateral proves hard to realize. Enforcement may also be done by large creditors (Chen 2013a). The large creditors of listed SOEs are the big four banks which are similarly state-owned (SOBs). Accordingly, it is very difficult for such banks to avoid both adverse selection and moral hazard in their lending practices to listed SOEs, due to heavy government intervention at multiple levels of deconcentration, even leaving room for possibilities of cronyism.

SOBs play a critical role at multiple levels in the malfunctioning of the stock market (Chen 2013a). They are a major source of the soft budget constraint; being listed, they themselves represent a very sizeable share of the stock index; their income mainly comes from interest margins, fattened by low deposit interest rates—acting as an incentive for investors to search for alternative opportunities in the stock (or real estate) market-; and weak internal control of banks imply that their loans often end up, through various channels, invested in the stock market.

In some markets where the state has given up control, the transactions are carried out through private networks. One important reason is that, as reviewed in Chap. 2, it is a tradition in China for contracting parties, instead of using the legal system and relying on the courts, to use their social network (*guanxi*) to enforce contracts (Granovetter 1985). In other words, instead of using formal and universal rules and regulations that govern individual behaviour, members in a social group rely on a web of personal ties and obey its rituals and mutual obligations that are informal and situation specific (Fei 1992; Faure 2006). Therefore, the weak legal system and the *guanxi*-based practices prevent business transactions from being at arm's length, further slowing down market development. Since institutional constraints prevent the formation of formal governance systems, *guanxi* may remain a crucial informal substitute. Stakeholders (business partners, customers, investors, lenders, and suppliers) extensively use network ties to engage in business transactions with the firms. More efforts should be devoted to understanding what roles social networks play in the corporate governance and transfer of information of China's listed firms. It may be wise for policy setters to try and get a better grasp of the value of these network ties and not rush to restrict too readily the widespread use of informal contracting and governance mechanisms (Wong 2016).

Alongside the administrative government apparatus and the SASAC controlled state-shareholding, listed firms are subject to a third source of control, via the organization of the Party (Yu 2013; on the financial industry, Heilmann 2005; Allen and Li 2018). The larger the number of employees in the SOE, the more likely the firm is to have a powerful party secretary (i.e. also holding a management position). The major duties of the party secretary are to disseminate the principles of the party, and implement the policies or resolutions of the party within the firm.

Even though China to a large extent mimicked the formal governance regime of western market economies, such a regime remains largely incomplete as control rights which stem from equity positions are partitioned among different stakeholders (Pistor 2012). An alternative mode of governance has been at work, human resource management (HRM), coordinated by the Party which controls the career path of top-level cadres.[3] HRM acts now both as a substitute to direct state control, which was the rule until the late 1990s, and as a complement to the new formal mechanisms of control based on rules. The party's control over HRM intensified as the state apparatus loosened its direct control over the financial system, separated out different regulatory functions from the central bank's unitary system of control, and sold important stakes in formerly SOBs to non-state, including foreign, investors. The HRM appears to work effectively for maintaining control over, and stabilizing the financial system. Two decades ago Qian (1996) emphasized that the government exercises its ultimate control over SOEs through personnel selection and dismissal. Morck and Yeung (2014) argue that the party has come to resemble the meritocratic imperial civil service that governed China during the Qing Empire. Corporations' party secretaries and party committees have veto power over critical decisions, but exercise it only very selectively to help the CEO and board avoid deviating from party objectives.

In China, great efforts have been made in the 2000s (especially under the impetus of Ms Shi from Hong Kong as vice-chairwoman of CSRC, from 2001 to 2004) to improve corporate transparency via financial disclosure (Piotroski and Wong 2012). The improvements occurred in three dimensions. First progress has taken place in the financial reporting practices of listed firms, converging to high-quality globally accepted standards. Second the financial reporting penalties for directors, supervisors, and managers have become more serious. Third, there has been a substantial tightening of the financial reporting process, with compulsory appointment of independent directors, of an audit committee, as well as a better assessment of internal controls by listed firms, accompanied with limitations on insider trading.

Although Chinese financial reporting looks good 'on paper', and has slowly improved, the information environment of Chinese listed companies

---

[3] The scope and nature of decision making inside SOEs was regulated by an important document released in July 2010 (China Institute 2018) about TCOI (Three Critical and One Important Collective Decision-Making Policy) for decisions of four types: politically oriented situations; second mid- or senior-level appointments; corporate expansion or restructuring; and fourth the use of off-budget funds. The party committee should be consulted on any TCOI decision.

remains opaque (Piotroski 2014). Despite the market-based and contracting-based incentives for transparency, countervailing cultural, legal, and political incentives for opacity are numerous. These include: the desire to minimize political costs associated with reporting bad outcomes; the need to hide expropriation practices as well as rent-seeking behavior; the dominance of relationship-based contracting and social connections; and institutional arrangements that reduce the demand for information and high-quality audits. Accordingly China lags behind peer emerging and/or Asian countries in terms of corporate transparency. Since limited firm-specific information is incorporated into security prices, individual listed company returns show a very high degree of co-movement with market returns (Morck et al. 2000).

5.2.2   Concentration of Ownership

SOEs in China are not subject to shareholder control for three reasons (Wang 2014): a large share of Chinese companies are state-owned; the state acts both as a controlling shareholder and as a regulator; and the real control comes from the state, through general requirements on policy compliance and specific powers, such as the appointment of the senior executives of SOEs, and sometimes even control over the operations of these firms. The underdevelopment of market institutions can be viewed as one of the reasons why Chinese listed firms have a high concentration of ownership (Wong 2016). Besides, listed firms often belong to a corporate group that is either vertically integrated or diversified into various industries. At the other end of the spectrum access to natural and financial resources is heavily controlled by the State. Corporate groups are then formed because, in the absence of private markets for these scarce resources, such a structure can create internal markets for accessing and allocating these resources.

La Porta et al. (1998) argue that firms which operate in economies with weak investor protection tend to have high ownership concentration. Investors, who fear expropriation by corporate insiders, will avoid buying the shares of such companies, and vice versa. In China political economy factors and social norms determine the firms' ownership structure (Wong 2016). The state, as a large shareholder, has weak incentives to monitor managers, but strong ones to expropriate minority shareholders. The state has to rely on its agents to monitor. When such agents represent SASAC, which does not enjoy any cash-flow right on the firms, they should not be expected to have any incentive either to supervise or to gain information like the agents of private owners. These state-delegated agents may lack capability to monitor, due either to lack of expertise, or to the lack of ability of the major owner to appoint (remove) managers of firms. Besides, the lack of convergence of their cash-flow and control rights provides an incentive to large shareholders to abuse minority shareholders, by consuming private benefits.

Tunnelling (Friedman et al. 2003) is a frequent practice of both state-dominated and private listed firms, whereby parent companies siphon-off the funds raised by their subsidiary during initial (IPO) or seasoned equity (SEO) public offerings (Cheung et al. 2009; Aharony et al. 2010; Peng et al. 2011; Li et al. 2017). Post-IPO, China's companies' earnings on average fall sharply, compare to their pre-IPO level (Allen et al. 2014; see Sect. 5.3). Such a drop in performance can be generated by the transfer of profits from the listed company to its group company, for instance through the lack of repayment of corporate loans, while the true performance of the listed company remains unchanged.[4] Empirical evidence on this phenomenon is provided by Allen et al. (2014), who computed, over a large sample of firms, the average operating performance of listed firms in China from three years before, to three years after, their IPO year. They find that Returns on Assets (ROA) of listed SOEs are the same than those of matched private firms during the three years before listing but drop to half that level from the IPO year onwards, while ROA remains stable for private firms.

Large shareholders are also strongly capable of expropriating minority ones, since the former dominate shareholders' general meetings, which have an impressive range of powers in China (Chen 2013a). Such meetings elect the board of directors, which is thus very often controlled by the state, due to concentrated ownership. The board of supervisors has only powers on paper and is composed either of government officials (for SOEs) or members with proximity to the largest private shareholder. Finally, independent directors are hardly effective, mostly depend on controlling shareholders who nominate most of them, and are in no position to challenge large shareholders or impose their will, and are not truly accountable. Ownership concentration is one of the strongest factors

[4] The presence of an internal capital market within a group is more frequent among local, rather than central, SOEs, and among state-owned, rather than private firms in China (He et al. 2013). Comparative evidence for 90 countries including China is provided by Gugler et al. (2012).

shaping the performance of firms, both in terms of profitability and efficiency.[5] The role of ownership concentration has been rising in China, in line with increased competition in markets.

In mature capital markets a high concentration of shares is not good, and many large international companies do not have a single controlling shareholder. However, the A-share market is exactly the opposite. Generally speaking, most A-share listed companies have a state-owned controlling shareholder (holding more than 50% of the shares), and only a few listed companies implement a decentralized equity governance structure. Such a controlling shareholder can basically decide everything, making the shareholders' meeting only symbolic. The misuse of the assets of listed companies, and the sale of junk assets to such companies at high prices, are commonplace among listed companies with controlling shareholders.

Such drawbacks of a single controlling shareholder seem to be common. Because of the lack of information disclosure, minority shareholders are not informed about the actions of the controlling shareholder. Even if they were informed, the minority shareholders would not have enough power to stop the illegal activities of controlling shareholders, especially for large state-owned ones. By contrast, a dispersal of shares would mean that the shareholders' meeting would truly become the highest authority of the company; they would be able to fully exercise corporate governance and, to a certain extent, prevent large shareholders from bullying small and medium-sized ones. Another benefit of a diversified share structure is that financial data would be relatively authentic. In addition, due to the diversification of equity, the large shareholder would not hold more shares, would have no motive to use its own resources to give the listed company a fake profit margin, and there would be no way to encroach on the profits of listed companies without the other shareholders being aware of it. The company's cash dividends would become more important for the large shareholder.

In the 1990s, there were so-called nothing-of-three stocks, that is, stocks for which there was no major state shareholder, no major legal

---

[5] The negative effects of ownership concentration on firm performance in China are documented by Hu et al. (2010). For publicly-traded firms in China, ownership concentration seems to be the major factor behind profitability and efficiency (Guthrie et al. 2007). This result is valid even when controlling for dominant ownership type. The rise in ownership concentration associated with the rise of SASAC positively affected the performance of SOEs under its control (Wang et al. 2011).

person shareholder, and no major foreign shareholder. The largest shareholder of such firms generally did not hold more than 20% of the stocks. These listed companies with relatively diversified shareholding structure were basically running smoothly, and there were few scandals. The issue of controlling shareholders has become topical again in the last few years, with a desire to prevent too much concentration of ownership.

A diversified shareholder structure may encounter many unexpected events, such as hostile acquisitions. The diversification of the share structure may also offer the possibility to discontinue the operation of listed companies. In the 2015–2017 Vanke equity fight, Shi Wang (president) and Liang Yu (general manager) both left the company, and Vanke's business strategy was affected. Of course, thanks to the diversification of Vanke's shareholding structure, its former large shareholder, China Resources Group (SOE), could not seize the assets of its listed companies. This may not be what China Resources Group wanted, but other shareholders did not agree.

On September 30, 2018, the China Securities Regulatory Commission (CSRC) issued the revised 'Code of Corporate Governance for Listed Companies'. This first major revision of the code since 2002 includes five major aspects. First, it strengthens the cash dividend of listed companies, and clearly defines the profit distribution method. Second, it strengthens the constraints on the controlling shareholders, the actual controllers and their related parties, and pays more attention to the protection of small- and medium-sized investors. Third, it promotes the participation of institutional investors in corporate governance and reinforces the role of the audit committee of the board of directors. Fourth, it puts forward new requirements for the stability of control rights faced by listed companies, the performance of independent directors, the incentive mechanisms of listed companies' managers, and the strength of information disclosure. Fifth, it reinforces the leading role of listed companies in environmental protection and social responsibility.

Based on the revision of the Code by the CSRC, the government has realized the shortcomings of corporate governance of Chinese listed companies and is determined to address them. Although the new Code points out the problems, much will depend on its enforcement. Although the CSRC has indicated that it will study and improve relevant regulations in accordance with the new Code, how to implement and enforce these standards may be a challenge for the government and regulators.

5.2.3   IPO Quota System

In the absence of formal legal protection of shareholders, China did not meet the same difficulties as other transitional economies in the governance of firms because it chose to adopt a quota system for IPOs. In China, administrative governance would thus have been a substitute for formal legal governance. The quota system represented an incentive for regional competition and the deconcentration of information collection for IPOs. The administrative governance structure built around the quota system fulfilled two major functions. First it mitigated the large-scale information problems faced by both investors and regulators in an economy in transition. Second, it generated incentives for government officials at the local level to choose 'viable' companies as candidates for IPOs.

Pistor and Xu (2005) argue that, under the quota system, the owners of the firms, that is, the local governments and central ministries, were assigned the responsibility of collecting and verifying information with regards to the firms. In order to compete with other localities in economic performance,[6] which is crucial for their career advancement, local bureaucrats had an incentive to select companies that were more viable to list. Indeed, good performance of the listed companies could bring more quotas (i.e. more equity finance) to the province, while delisting or forced bailout would tarnish their economic performance records. The quota system functioned as an alternative to legal protection of shareholders rights.

The weaknesses of the quota system are emphasized by Chen (2013a), who, challenging Pistor and Xu (2005), argues that the latter overestimated the importance of equity finance to local economies, misunderstood the role of the Chinese stock market, and overrated the credibility of the punishment for choosing wrong companies. It would be incorrect to assume that local officials had no other personal interest in the selection process, and one should not forget that the quota system was a source of rent-seeking and corruption. This alternative view would imply that the quota system often led to the listing of the wrong companies and provincial officials may have helped many firms fake their entire financial histories. Due to inherent weaknesses, the system did not prove sustainable and was later abandoned.

---

[6] Deconcentration and inter-jurisdiction competition is a factor put forward by Xu (2011) as one of the drivers of rapid growth in China in the 1980s and 1990s.

5.3   Multiple Principals and Price Informativeness

Existing literature has rightly perceived some dimensions of the complexity of the environment of Chinese listed SOEs, involving multiple principals. It has also partly emphasized the role of local governments, but only focused on one level: provinces. We consider that a full understanding of that complexity requires a two-step analysis, which first disentangles the interactions inside a web of state institutions appearing as multiple principals, and second, demonstrates how this game is not restricted to the central level, but made much more complex by the interactions of the various deconcentrated levels of government.

According to Carpenter et al. (2015), the Chinese stock market would have become able to value firms in an appropriate way, akin to the US stock market.[7] This diagnostics is based on a test of price informativeness, which verifies that current stock prices of listed firms reflect their future earnings. The specification they use is borrowed from the work by Bai et al. (2016), carried out on US firms' data, which regresses[8] the current Earnings over Book-value-over-assets ratio (E/A), on its own lagged value and the lagged Market value over book-value-of-assets ratio (M/A). Carpenter et al. (2015) argue that the average value of the effect of lagged (M/A) on current (E/A), estimated with annual cross-sectional data, for China, is similar to that found in the US. However, in the case of China it is important to explain the way in which each, among the three, component is controlled by a different principal, with no immediate interest in the other variables.[9]

Earnings, in their gross (but not in their net of interest) form, are controlled by the company's chief executive officer (CEO). The central or

---

[7] For earlier evidence on the link between accounting information and firms' stock returns, see Chen et al. (2001).

[8]
$$E/A = a + b(M/A)_{-1} + c(E/A)_{-1}$$
(5.1)

where E, A, and M, respectively, refer to earnings, the book value of assets, and market value.

[9] We will not dwell here on the fact that this specification may be questionable from an econometric point of view. First, in terms of time series modelling, it leaves aside common factors across firms (a la Market model) and does not deal with the likely non-stationarity of the data. Second, due to many missing variables (such as changes in economic growth), it is very likely that coefficient b is overestimated. In contrast, market value should be filtered from factors which are unlikely to be linked to future earnings. The latter would raise coefficient b.

local government can tell CEOs to use their net earnings to invest in some other sector or location. We thus expect E and M to be disconnected in China. Political economy factors are likely to impact both M, the market value of firms, which is driven by CSRC and the People's Bank of China (PBoC), and earnings dynamics, itself driven by SASAC, the State Council, and the National Development and Reform Commission (NDRC). Besides, M and E are driven by orthogonal factors. Moreover, the autoregressive coefficient of (E/A) is likely to be strongly biased by the smoothing of earnings and tunnelling. It is all the more surprising that this autoregressive coefficient is not reported by Carpenter et al. (2015). The CEOs of large SOEs care about E because it determines their promotion/demotion by SASAC.

In the primary market, it looks like the regulator (CSRC) is the key player but on the demand side, as well as the supply side, other ministries are involved. There is a strong selection bias in the choice of firm to be listed at the time of both IPOs (and similarly for SEOs). Such a bias is the product of complex interactions between principals with divergent interests. Initially the yearly IPO listing quota (i.e. the ceiling of issuance obtained as the product of the IPO price times the number of shares times the number of companies) was the major tool used by both the State Council and the CSRC for the rationing of share supply (see Fig. 5.1.). This also allows the regulator to suspend IPOs whenever the market is judged too depressed, a suspension which can very well last several years.

During the reform process of SOEs, the hardening of the budget constraint, putting an end to the unlimited availability of low-cost bank credit, generated a potentially unlimited demand for listing on the part of all companies. Initially the IPO quotas were aimed at curbing this demand, via a rationing system. Multiple objectives pursued with only one instrument (IPO and SEO quotas) must sometimes be in conflict because they are unrelated. The under-pricing of IPOs was both a way to indirectly enforce the hard budget constraint on firms and make IPOs more attractive to investors.

Indeed, before 2007, there was typically a post-IPO jump in price, but since then, for giant listed companies, there has been a price fall post-IPO. In other words, initially the listing price of IPOs was too low and then too high. Why would you set a low listing price[10]? CSRC usually sets the listing

---

[10] The literature on IPO underpricing in China is surveyed for 63 studies by Azevedo et al. (2018). The evolution of IPO procedures and pricing is reviewed by Su and Yu (2015).

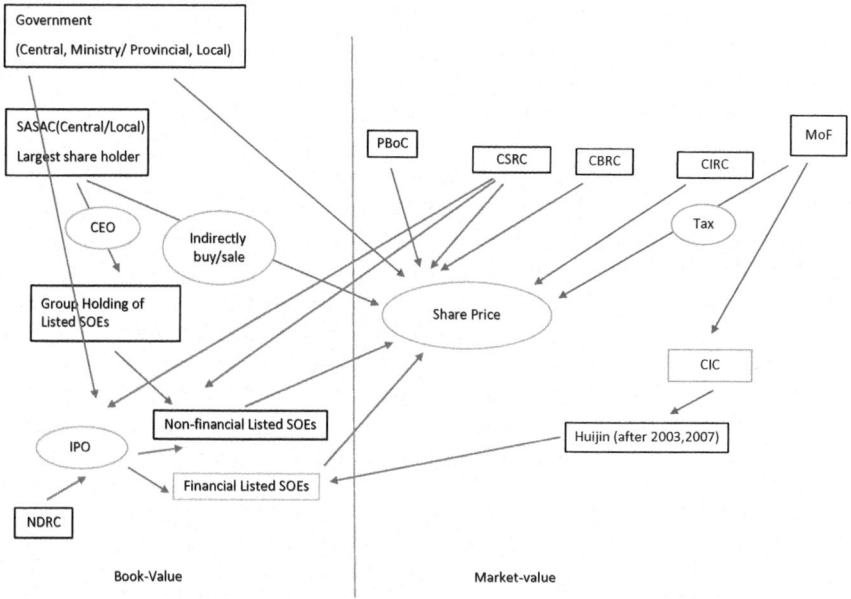

Fig. 5.1 Principals involved in setting the book value and the market value. The same structure is replicated at all major levels of decentralization, not overlapping with geographical regions. Acronyms in the chart are defined as follows: Chief Executive Officer (CEO), China's Banking Regulatory Commission (CBRC), China Investment Corporation (CIC), China's Insurance Regulatory Commission (CIRC), China's Security and Regulatory Commission (CSRC), initial public offering (IPO), ministry of finance (MOF), ministry of justice (MOJ), National Development and Reform Commission (NDRC), People's Bank of China (PBoC), State-owned enterprises (SOEs), Supervision and Administration Commission of the State Council (SASAC)

price on the basis of prices of similar firms in the relevant industry. When giant firms came to be listed on the stock market they wanted to raise a lot of money but large investors did not want to buy these shares, because they could not corner the market for such high-capitalization shares. A low IPO price was necessary to attract investors. The cap on intra-day movements of post-IPO prices was set by CSRC in 2014 at 44% on the first day, and 10% after the IPO day. For small companies the post-IPO rise in the price used to be persistent.

In the secondary market, the movements in the share prices, reflected in the market value (M), are also influenced by the authorities, in a variety of ways. In a direct way the Exchange sets intra-day price caps. In an indirect way the PBoC decides on aggregate liquidity, with the involvement of the China Banking Regulatory Commission (CBRC) for its distribution. In addition, the government controls a substantial part of institutional investors' demand and supply of shares. This involves the China Insurance Regulatory Commission (CIRC) in the case of insurance companies.

Reaching the listing stage is as difficult for private firms as for SOEs. In the pre-listing process, the behaviour of the former is no different from that of the latter, with a bundling of assets, except that the decision process seems much more direct. Accordingly, the private dimension is yet another layer on top of the geographically deconcentrated and ministerial, etc., levels. An added feature is that the pressure on key decision-makers may not be limited to gentle lobbying but may also involve some attempts at corruption.

SASAC was very powerful in the selection of the bundle of assets to be combined into a candidate firm for listing. It is also heavily involved in the valuation of this selection of assets.[11] After an IPO, SASAC was also very concerned with monitoring that managers take as their preferred objective the maximization of the book value of the assets, again not at the level of the listed company but for the whole group, possibly at the expense of earnings.

SASAC does not want to influence the market value, but it may need to rethink its rule. It could take care of, and even possibly intervene in, the market. This possibility may not be activated since there is strong resistance among government circles to start selling shares of the large SOEs which are state property. SASAC is the biggest institutional investor, but it has only a buy-and-hold strategy. It could have a symmetric strategy, both buying and selling, to aim at making capital gains on its assets, acting itself as yet another arm of China's sovereign wealth fund, and regulate share prices, acting as stabilizer.

Large SOEs were restructured to make them more market-oriented ('efficient'). Companies were created, whose assets were previously under direct management by various ministries, such as China Telecom under the Ministry of Communications, China Railway under the Ministry of

---

[11] SASAC attempts to harvest dividends from the companies under its remit are well tracked by Naughton (2008).

Transport, and China Post under the Ministry of Post. Then quasi-holding companies were created, embedding several SOEs, such as the group company including Sinopec and China Petroleum. Inside the group, the good assets were selected to make a bundle offered for listing in an IPO. The other members of the group included bad assets, activities unrelated to those in the listed company, or social activities. The group companies were truly in control of all major decisions and represented a single entity, inside which profits could move, via transfer pricing from the listed company to the group, or loans granted by the group to the listed company, typically used to do window dressing before seasoned equity offerings, etc. The CEO of the group company is at a very high official rank, such as minister or vice-minister level, and thus much higher than the CEO of the listed company. Accordingly, the listed company had no choice but to comply with the group directives. The listing itself was intended as a way to put pressure on the SOEs to become more market oriented, thanks to the supposed control offered by shareholders' governance, plus information disclosure to shareholders and regulators, and to provide a low-cost source of financing.

Listed SOEs are in some way only the tip of the iceberg. They appear in the shop window but are not really representative of what is going on in state-sector firms. They are neither the most profitable, nor the most efficient. Their assets are rather put together under the label of a firm so as to appear the most attractive, as well as the most consensual, given the multiple principals involved in the decision to list them. Indeed, the IPO phase is only the last phase in a survival-of-the-fittest contest in which the 'firm' has to successfully go through multiple filters. The group's assets generally include huge undisclosed (contingent) liabilities on top of the listed companies' assets. All in all, this implies that the denominator in the Carpenter et al. (2015) price-informativeness equation should be the book value of the group's assets rather than the listed firm's ones.

Before the split-share reform (SSR) the major focus of SASAC was on the asset selection and valuation prior to SOE's IPOs. This explains why the left-hand-side of Fig. 5.1. was so important. After the split-share reform, SASAC's focus moved away from the pre-IPO process to supervising the daily operations of listed giant SOEs.

A very specific feature of the Chinese stock market is the irreversibility of listing. Indeed, in spite of its legal existence, delisting is hardly ever activated. Badly performing firms can be blacklisted, when classified as under 'special treatment' or 'particular transfer', but neither of those treatments prevents their shares from being quoted.

5.4   Deconcentrated Multiple Principals of Listed SOEs

The complexity of the agency problems in corporate governance is enhanced by the spatial dimension associated to what is generally referred to as decentralization, but may more properly be called deconcentration,[12] in China. Indeed, it cannot be assumed that the central government, represented by SASAC is itself fully in control of SOEs under its arm. There is a conflict of objectives between SASAC and deconcentrated local principals (Siqueira et al. 2009). Multiple principals face a single agent which performs multiple tasks (as in the multitask theory of Chinese SOEs, see Chap. 3). Multiple local principals represent various local authorities that interact with the SOEs and influence their decisions. The diverse local players include the four levels of deconcentration (provinces, cities, and counties), while the central principal is SASAC. The local principals value social harmony, while SASAC values efficiency or the book value of assets. In other words, the multiplicity of principals in the agency process is not limited to the central level but replicated at different levels of jurisdictions.

The complexity of the reform, and of the subsequent functioning, of the listed firms in China is contained in the specificities of the selective privatization process. Indeed, most geographical levels of government control a set of SOEs. Each of these levels intended to privatize according to the 'seize the big and release the small' policy, which resulted in four sets of Swiss cheese with different hole sizes.

The deconcentration of the control of firms among the four levels of jurisdictions was inherited from the planning system. However, the privatization thresholds came into conflict with such deconcentration. Each jurisdiction level followed the letter of the privatization mantra: selecting its own small fish for privatization and keeping its own large ones, which, at the higher level of jurisdiction, would have been privatized. Accordingly, the number of privatized firms became much smaller than what the central

[12] Deconcentration refers to the dispersion of control within one single organization, while decentralization refers to the transfer of control from one organization to another (Lemieux 2008; Aritonang 2016). This can be linked to the distinction made by Gu Yanwu between *Junxian* and *Fengjian* in his 1660 essay on the prefectural system (see Kuhn 1975).

authorities had intended in the first place. Actually, it was even more restricted, since the lower-level jurisdiction claimed priority in grabbing control of so-called small fish at the immediately higher level of jurisdiction, which should have been privatized. As a result, very few SOEs would have been privatized. Eventually the central government understood these unintended consequences and compelled lower-level jurisdictions to privatize the true small fish. This experience provides a hint of the multiple principal-agent problems which are at the core of the difficulties faced by the stock market in China.

Deconcentration has been a very long-lasting feature of the Chinese economy, part and parcel of the imperial system. The deconcentration pattern is replicated at each and every (or most) level(s) of the regulatory and control structure. The local head of SASAC reports both to the local government and to the higher-level SASAC head, but possibly more to the former than to the latter. Indeed, local interest may dominate for major decisions. Each among the four geographically deconcentrated SASACs is in control of all the state-owned assets at its level of jurisdiction. It appoints the CEO of the group concerned but is also involved in management decisions, the choice of entity to be listed, the order of listing, as well as the exclusion of some companies from that process.

Local bureaus at the Ministry of Finance (MOF) are also heavily involved in the listing process. They carefully monitor both the destination and the use of the financial proceeds of the listing, and, most of the time, transfer them to the listed firm. However, nothing prevents them from using part of such proceeds for other purposes, possibly inside the group to which the firm belongs, or to fund local authorities' investment projects. Again, we find the multiple-principals process at work since the local MOF bureau chief is accountable both to his (rarely her) higher-level jurisdiction boss at MOF and to the local official at the same jurisdiction level. The local MOF is also the accounting office of all the activities of the local government. When the listed company distributes dividends, technically, for state-owned shares the proceeds go to the central or local MOF. The latter can then decide to allocate them to whatever use it wants to make. Anyway, this is always small scale given the limited profitability of many SOEs.

NDRC is in charge of industrial policy, which entitles it to be involved in granting the permission for an IPO, and, in coordination with SASAC, to decide on the composition of the asset bundle to be listed. Activities which were initially in charge of the NDRC were subsequently spun off into SASAC. Indeed, in 1988 SASAC was only a bureau of NDRC, and became a separate institution when merged with some bureaus of MOF.

As implied by the above, the local official (provincial governor, city mayor or county head) is the *de facto* boss of all the local heads of SASAC, MOF, and NDRC, making him (rarely her) the most powerful official in the jurisdiction. The structure is of course doubled at each and every level by the party secretaries.

Financial regulators had to be made relatively independent of local governments in order to be insulated from pressures by the latter. Such regulators now have their own deconcentrated structure, with regional offices whose geographical spans do not necessarily correspond with those of the levels of deconcentrated jurisdictions. The central PBoC, CSRC, CBRC, and CIRC, all appoint the heads of their regional offices. Each of them has its own deconcentrated structure with districts which rarely match. This adds further to the complexity of the multiple-principals pattern. Due to competition among local authorities, PBoC has increased its number of offices to the point where there is almost one per province.

The CBRC needs to approve the issuance of asset management products (by hedge funds in particular), but it has no direct involvement in the listing process. Though initially the CSRC was a department of the PBoC (so its creation was similar to the spin-off of SASAC from NDRC), it was separated from the latter in 1995, and subsequently became deputy minister level, while PBoC is at a more senior (i.e. ministry) level. Usually the chairman of CSRC is either a former vice-chairman of PBoC or a former president of one of the four SOBs. In periods of market turmoil, liquidity creation by PBoC can become a critical factor, either to help hinder speculative activities or revive a bear market.

The CSRC is one of the multiple principals involved in controlling the quota and price of IPOs and determines which firms can be listed, when, and for which amount. It also has an indirect influence on the choice of asset bundles submitted to it for listing. CSRC's regional offices number 36, thus including not only the number and span of provinces and autonomous cities, but also some extra cities. It is not only each and every province but also each and every ministry which is keen to have its own listed companies. Ministries like to build up group companies, thus at the ministry level, in order to increase the employment of officials, and get some proceeds of listings. Stock market listing is thus also a means of preserving social harmony, and CSRC has to balance these divergent and conflicting interests.

The CBRC and CIRC are involved in the listing of banks and insurance companies respectively. In addition, the former is involved in liquidity provision issues, while the latter's involvement stems from the fact that insurance companies are one of the major institutional investors in the stock market.

A typical sequence in the process leading to a listing could be described as follows. First a city government, with no listed company yet, after consulting with the local SASAC, would put together a ready-made bundle of assets which it proposes as a candidate firm for listing, in competition with similar proposals by its peers in other cities. Second, the provincial government in which those cities are located would decide which one among these proposals is going to be selected. The provincial government itself may have its own proposals for listing. After making up its mind on the short-listed companies, the provincial government would have to respect a quota, often implicit, set by CSRC at the national level. One way to maximize the chances of the province's proposal to get through would be for the provincial official to approach one ministry at the central government and propose that one of the province's candidates be included in that ministry's implicit listing quota. Third, the choice of the company to be selected for listing did not simply depend on its performance and characteristics but was also very strongly influenced by this extremely complex and competitive process inside the multi-layered bureaucratic decision-making system. Heavy lobbying by the provincial/city governments was involved. Horizontal and vertical dimensions played a key role in the multi-principals game. It may have been as difficult for a company to be granted the right to list, as for a student coming from a remote province to be admitted to Peking University.

Why would the city government want to have one of its firms listed? Two series of reasons are involved. First, as mentioned above, the promotion of local officials depends on the number of companies listed in his (or her) jurisdiction, which testifies on their achievements (alongside the local growth rate...), and the listing process provides resources which will boost growth. Second, local governments face many burdens, some of them economic, such as employment or pensions, in order to maintain social harmony. To finance such extra tasks they need extra resources. All this provides very strong incentives to local governments to achieve new listings. At the city level, the mayor is the true local CEO. As seen above, there are multiple principals together with (often) multiple agents, and some of them are alternatively one or the other. The legal department of the local government may also be involved in the listing decision. Besides, local governments can also transfer resources to a company after listing, for the latter to do some window-dressing before SEOs.

5.5   Summary and Conclusions

Many features of China's stock market, uncovered by extensive empirical work carried out by western researchers, using seasoned methodology of best-practice or frontier finance developed and refined for OECD countries' stock markets, are seen as puzzles. However, in the light of our political-economy analysis above, these features appear as expected outcomes, as reflected in the point of view of seasoned practitioners of China's stock market and its state-owned system. Such features indeed stem from two Chinese characteristics: the large number of idiosyncratic enforcement mechanisms at work in corporate governance, and the interaction of multiple principals which manipulate many key market variables.

The latest western research on China's stock market has left unaddressed some key questions (Carpenter and Whitelaw 2017) to which our analysis provides some tentative answers. There are two main series of open or pending issues. The first ones refer to the cost of funding and the efficiency of capital allocation. The second ones relate to investors' strategies in terms of domestic and foreign portfolio allocation.

With respect to the first series of issues, SOEs have much easier access to bank loans than private firms. They pay relatively high interest rates on these loans but then make private firms bear the burden in a number of ways, including inter-firm loans at higher rates, or reverse margins charged to their private suppliers. With respect to tapping the stock market, SOEs have a much easier access to listing than private firms. Since dividends are rarely distributed, state-owned companies use the stock market as a free lunch to get funding. This justified the use by the authorities of a quota system for IPOs. With the reform of the financial system, the burden for the private sector may be lightened. Share prices do not provide signals able to guide an efficient allocation of capital, which anyway is not a direct goal of the government. Its true goal is to use the stock market to enhance the role of SOEs, their governance, and supervision, on top of funding them.

A major change in focus took place in the mid-2000s. Prior to this date the focus was on the listing process, that is, the primary market, while subsequently it moved to the secondary market, essentially after the listing of the very large SOEs (and partly after the split-share reform). Accordingly, IPO reform is no more urgent, and is less important than what many western observers think, to improve the efficiency of the allocation of capital. There are already about 3500 listed companies in China's stock market, a number close to the US. IPO reform would not by itself change the corporate governance of listed firms, the improvement of which should be a priority for the future. Another priority should be the reform of many large SOEs, making transparent the hands-on approach to control by the government. Government domination or intervention will not disappear in China's stock market in a short period of time, but as the stock market matures on the investors' side, as well as in terms of enforcement, information disclosure and corporate governance, the government should consider whether it truly wants to increase the role of the market.

With respect to the second series of open issues, constraints on portfolio diversification for Chinese domestic household investors are overwhelming. It is not possible for such households to buy government bonds, and they can hardly (though increasingly) access foreign-listed securities. The portfolio of household investors has gradually been allowed to diversify away from an exclusive reliance on bank deposits (with negative real return, but the lowest risk), to share trading 30 years ago (with zero long-run real return), and to real estate investment 20 years ago (with positive real return, and low risks given the buy-and-hold investment strategy of most households). Institutional investors have been allowed and they have grown fast, but they are constrained to stick to a buy-and-hold strategy for shares and suffer from the lack of short-selling instruments, often preventing them from playing a stabilizing role.

China's stock market is an opportunity for diversification of global portfolios. From the point of view of global investors with a medium-run horizon the inclusion of A-shares in the MSCI Emerging Markets (and other) index(es) was a timely decision. From the point of view of foreign investors with a much longer horizon, many uncertainties stem from the extent of the government's intention to use the stock market to achieve its own interests. International investors should understand that timing their entry and exit is important, due to the uniqueness of China's stock market. If the timing is chosen well, a foreign investor may get a very good medium-term return on investment. But a simple long-term buy-and-hold strategy will hardly be profitable, because of the lack of regular dividend distribution (generally disconnecting the stock market from the real economy), the absence of profit maximization as the main objective of listed companies, and the alternation of bear and speculative phases. In terms of international risk sharing, given the low correlation between China's and foreign markets, investing in A-shares will enable these global investors to spread risk. Still, the gain in terms of the return-risk (Sharpe) ratio depends very much on the length of holding of their investment.

On the face of it, it may seem that the stock market would be one of the main sources of financial instability in China. From a different perspective, the stock market may play a stabilizing role since it absorbs a lot of excess liquidity, and speculative stock market waves do not seem to spill over much to the real economy.

We believe that China's stock market development and functioning are complex political economy issues inherently involving multiple principals. There is a tension between reform and liberalization on the one side, and stabilization and keeping control[13] on the other, as well as a need to balance these conflicting objectives, in which different interest groups would like to be favoured. These are the most important issues which should be studied in further research on China's stock market.

REFERENCES

Aharony, J., J. Wang, and H. Yuan. 2010. Tunnelling as an Incentive for Earnings Management During the IPO Process. *Journal of Accounting and Public Policy* 29: 1–26.

Allen, F. 2001. Do Financial Institutions Matter? *Journal of Finance* 56: 1165–1175.

Allen, J., and R. Li. 2018. Awakening Governance: The Evolution of Corporate Governance in China, Asian Corporate Governance Association, Report, Hong Kong.

Allen, F., J. Qian, and M. Qian. 2005. Law, Finance, and Economic Growth in China. *Journal of Financial Economics* 77: 57–116.

Allen, F., J. Qian, S.C. Shan, and J.L. Zhu. 2014. The Best Performing Economy with the Worst Performing Stock Market: Explaining the Poor Performance of the Chinese Stock Market. Manuscript, Imperial College, University of London.

Allen W.T., and H. Shen. 2011. Assessing China's Top-Down Securities Markets. NBER Working Paper, 16713.

Aritonang, D.M. 2016. Politics of Deconcentration for Local Government: The Case of Indonesia. *Journal of Law, Policy and Globalization* 55: 79–86.

---

[13] Conflicts of objectives in state enterprise reform in China are well analyzed by Naughton (2017).

Azevedo, A., Y. Guney, and J. Leng. 2018. Initial Public Offerings in China: Underpricing, Statistics and Developing Literature. *Research in International Business and Finance* 46: 387–398.

Bai, J., T. Philippon, and A. Savov. 2016. Have Financial Markets Become More Informative. *Journal of Financial Economics* 122 (3): 625–654.

Carpenter, J.N., F. Lu, and R.F. Whitelaw. 2015. The Real Value of China's Stock Market. NBER Working Paper, 20957.

Carpenter, J.N., and R.F. Whitelaw. 2017. The Development of China's Stock Market and Stakes for the Global Economy. *Annual Review of Financial Economics* 9: 233–257.

Cheffins, B. 2003. Law as Bedrock: The Foundations of an Economy Dominated by Widely Held Public Companies. *Oxford Journal of Legal Studies* 23 (1): 1–23.

Chen, Z. 2003. Capital Markets And Legal Development: The China Case. *China Economic Review* 14 (4): 451–472.

Chen, D. 2013a. *Corporate Governance Enforcement and Financial Development: The Chinese Experience*. Cheltenham: Edward Elgar.

———. 2013b. Developing a Stock Market Without Institutions: The China Puzzle. *Journal of Corporate Law Studies*: 151–184.

Chen, J.P., S. Chen, and X. Su. 2001. Is Accounting Information Value-Relevant in the Emerging Chinese Stock Market? *Journal of International Accounting, Auditing and Taxation* 10: 1–22.

Cheung, Y.-L., L. Jing, P.R. Rau, and A. Stouraitis. 2009. Tunnelling and Propping up: An Analysis of Related Party by Chinese Companies. *Pacific Basin Finance Journal* 17: 372–393.

China Institute. 2018. State-owned Enterprises in the Chinese Economy Today: Role, Reform, and Evolution, University of Alberta, Report.

Coffee, J. 2001. The Rise of Dispersed Ownership: The Roles of Law and the States in the Separation of Ownership and Control. *Yale Law Journal* 111: 1–82.

Fan, J.P.H., and R. Morck, eds. 2012. *Capitalizing China*. Chicago: Chicago University Press.

Faure, D. 2006. *China and Capitalism: A History of Business Enterprise in Modern China*. Hong Kong: Hong Kong University Press.

Fei, X. 1992. *From the Soil: The Foundations of Chinese Society*. Translated by G.G. Hamilton and Z. Wang. Oakland: University of California Press.

Friedman, E., S. Johnson, and T. Mitton. 2003. Propping and Tunnelling. *Journal of Comparative Economics* 31: 732–750.

Granovetter, M. 1985. Economic Action and Social Structure: The Problem of Embeddedness. *American Journal of Sociology* 91 (3): 481–510.

Gugler, K., E. Peev, and E. Segalla. 2012. The Internal Workings of Internal Capital Markets. *Journal of Corporate Finance* 20: 59–73.

Guthrie, D., Z. Xiao, and J. Wang. 2007. Aligning the Interests of Multiple Principals: Ownership Concentration and Profitability in China's Publicly Traded Companies. Working Paper, EX-07-32, New York University, Stern School of Business.

He, J., X. Mao, O.M. Rui, and X. Zha. 2013. Business Groups in China. *Journal of Corporate Finance* 22: 166–192.

Heilmann, S. 2005. Regulatory Innovation by Leninist Means: Party Supervision in China's Financial Industry. *China Quarterly* 181: 1–21.

Hu, H.W., O.K. Tam, and M.G.-S. Tan. 2010. Internal Governance Mechanisms and Firm Performance in China. *Asia Pacific Journal of Management* 27: 727–749.

Jones, W.C. 2003. Trying to Understand the Current Chinese Legal System. In *Understanding China's Legal System: Essays in Honor of Jerome A. Cohen*, ed. C.S. Hsu. New York: New York University Press.

Kuhn, P.A. 1975. Local Self-government Under the Republic: Problems of Controls, Autonomy and Mobilization. In *Conflict and Control in Late imperial China*, ed. F. Wakeman Jr. and C. Grant, 257–298. Berkeley: University of California Press.

Lemieux, V. 2008. Deconcentration and Decentralization: A Question of Terminology. *Canadian Public Administration* 29 (2): 318–323.

Li, K., L. Lu, J. Qian, and L. Zhu. 2017. Enforceability and the Effectiveness of Law and Regulation. Working Paper, China Academy of Financial Research.

Li, L.W., and C.J. Milhaupt. 2013. We Are the (National) Champions: Understanding the Mechanisms of State Capitalism in China. *Stanford Law Review* 65 (4): 697–760.

Morck, R., and B. Yeung. 2014. Corporate Governance in China. *Journal of Applied Corporate Finance* 26 (3): 20–42.

Morck, R., B. Yeung, and W. Yu. 2000. The Information Content of Stock Markets: Why Do Emerging Markets Have Synchronous Price Movements. *Journal of Financial Economics* 58: 215–260.

Naughton, B. 2008. SASAC and Rising Corporate Power in China, Brookings Institution. *China Leadership Monitor* 24: 1–9.

———. 2017. The Current Wave of State Enterprise Reform in China: A Preliminary Appraisal. *Asian Economic Policy Review* 12: 282–298.

Peng, W.Q., K.C.J. Wei, and Z. Yang. 2011. Tunnelling or Propping: Evidence from Connected Transactions. *Journal of Corporate Finance* 17: 306–325.

Piotroski, J. 2014. Financial Reporting Practices of China's Listed Firms. *Journal of Applied Corporate Governance* 26 (3): 53–60.

Piotroski, J.D., and T.J. Wong. 2012. Institutions and Information Environment of Chinese Listed Firms. In *Capitalizing China*, ed. J.P.H. Fan and R. Morck, 201–214. Chicago: University of Chicago Press.

Pistor, K. 2012. The Governance of China's Finance. In *Capitalizing China*, ed. J.P.H. Fan and R. Morck, 35–60. Chicago: University of Chicago Press.

Pistor, K., and C. Xu. 2005. Governing Stock Markets in Transition Economies: Lessons from China. *American Law and Economics Review* 7 (1): 184–210.

La Porta, R., F. Lopez-De-Silanez, A. Schleifer, and R.W. Vishny. 1998. Law and finance. *Journal of Political Economy* 106: 1113–1155.

Qian, Y. 1996. Enterprise Reform in China: Agency Problems and Political Control. *Economics of Transition* 4 (2): 427–447.

Siqueira, K., T. Sandler, and J. Cauley. 2009. Common Agency and State-owned Enterprise Reform. *China Economic Review* 20: 208–217.

Su, C., and J. Yu. 2015. Market-oriented Reform of China's IPO System and Information Disclosure Regulations. In *The Chinese Stock Market*, ed. S. Cheng and Z. Li, vol. 1, 39–105. Basingstoke: Palgrave Macmillan.

Wang, J. 2014. The Political Logic of Corporate Governance in China's State-owned Enterprises. *Cornell International Law Journal* 47 (3): 631–665.

Wang, J., D. Guthrie, and Z. Xiao. 2011. The Rise of SASAC: Asset Management, Ownership Concentration and Firm Performance in China's Capital Markets. *Management and Organization Review* 8 (2): 253–281.

Weian, L., and H. Chen. 2015. Corporate Governance Evaluation Research of China's Listed Companies. In *The Chinese Stock Market*, ed. S. Cheng and Z. Li, vol. 2, 190–287. Basingstoke: Palgrave Macmillan.

Wong, T.J. 2016. Corporate Governance Research on Listed Firms in China. *Foundations and Trends in Accounting* 9 (4): 259–326.

Xu, C. 2011. The Fundamental Institutions of China's Reforms and Development. *Journal of Economic Literature* 49 (4): 1076–1151.

Yu, W. 2013. Party Control in China's Listed Firms. *Czech Journal of Economics and Finance* 63 (4): 382–397.

Zhang, Z. 2016. Law and Finance: The Case of Stock Market Development in China. *International and Comparative Law Review* 39: 283.

Index[1]

[1] Note: Page numbers followed by 'n' refer to notes.

© The Author(s) 2019
E. Girardin, Z. Liu, *Demystifying China's Stock Market*,
https://doi.org/10.1007/978-3-030-17123-0